Quantum Leaps in School Leadership

Perry R. Rettig

A SCARECROWEDUCATION BOOK

The Scarecrow Press, Inc.
Lanham, Maryland, and London
2002

A SCARECROWEDUCATION BOOK

Published in the United States of America
by Scarecrow Press, Inc.
A Member of the Rowman & Littlefield Publishing Group
4720 Boston Way, Lanham, Maryland 20706
www.scaroweducation.com

4 Pleydell Gardens, Folkstone
Kent CT20 2DN, England

British Library Cataloguing in Publication Information Available

Library of Congress Cataloging-in-Publication Data

Rettig, Perry Richard.
    Quantum leaps in school leadership / Perry R. Rettig.
        p. cm.
    "A Scarecrow education book."
    Includes bibliographical references and index.
    ISBN 0-8108-4400-1 (alk. paper)—ISBN 0-8108-4217-3 (pbk. : alk. paper)
    1. Educational leadership. 2. School management and organization. 3. Organizational
sociology. I. Title.

LB2806 .R44 2002
371.2—dc21

                                                                    2002018720

∞^{TM} The paper used in this publication meets the minimum requirements of
American National Standard for Information Sciences—Permanence of Paper for
Printed Library Materials, ANSI/NISO Z39.48-1992.
Manufactured in the United States of America.

This book is dedicated to my family. The support of Jan, Kelly, and Lisa have made this possible. The influence of my mother, Maxine, and the inspiration of my father, Marwood, have also made this possible. Finally, I dedicate this book to all the people who are searching for a more natural connection to their work.

Contents

0130776

List of Figures

Preface

Great spirits have always encountered violent opposition from
mediocre minds.

—Albert Einstein

The first premise of this book is that current leadership practices are
based upon the science of Newtonian physics. This approach is flawed
in that it is an inappropriate method to look at human, social, and dynamic systems. On the other hand, this classical approach is very appropriate for the study of closed systems like machines and clockwork
mechanisms. But as Margaret Wheatley (1994a, p. 29) posited, "A mechanical world feels distinctly anti-human." The second premise of
this book is that a model derived from lessons in quantum physics is
more appropriate. There is no math in this book. It is designed to be
read and used by any practicing school administrator or any person in
training for educational leadership. You don't have to be an expert in
quantum physics (of even have any background in it at all) to appreciate its importance in creating a new model for school change. Quantum physics is a set of scientific principles and approaches that is more
conducive to studying open systems, such as the ecology, social systems, and people. This author is not proposing that Newtonian or classical physics is wrong; it is a sound and credible science. However,
this science that spurred on the Industrial Revolution is not the science
to use to study leadership and dynamic systems. Ilya Prigogine and
Isabelle Stengers (1984, p. 2) wrote, "Our vision of nature is undergo-
ing a radical change toward the multiple, the temporal, and the complex." In terms of leadership, "When managers today produce successful change of any significance in organizations . . . the process is

time consuming and highly complex, never a one-two-three, hit-and-run affair" (Kotter, 1999, p. 7).

The traditional view is more rational, linear, and simple, whereas the new view is more intuitive, multifaceted, and complex. Again, the past view is more reductionistic and encourages competition, whereas the newer thinking is more holistic and encourages cooperation. Mathematics is the language of the sciences. Classical physics uses the quantitative mathematics of linear algebra, analytic geometry, and calculus. Quantum physics and the other new sciences use the qualitative mathematics of dynamic systems theory, topology geometry, and fractal geometry. In other words, the new sciences use the mathematics of relationships and patterns. Again, this book is intended for the lay reader, not the mathematician or scientist. It does, however, examine the key principles of these new sciences and then explores the implications for educational leadership.

Chapter 1 has the purpose of reviewing Newtonian physics, as well as its impact on traditional models of leadership in educational systems. Chapter 2 examines why this classical model is an inappropriate way to study leadership and why it's an inappropriate model for leadership.

Chapter 3 focuses on defining quantum physics in terms of describing the theory and associated concepts. Several theoretical and actual experiments will be explored. It also examines why a quantum physics model is more appropriate to study leadership and organizations like educational systems. Chapter 4 then takes a tangent away from quantum physics and looks at new research in other areas of science. In particular, work in chemistry, biology, neurobiology, ecology, the complexity sciences, and fractals will be investigated.

Finally, the last two chapters bring closure to this book. Chapter 5 neatly summarizes these new key concepts and the lessons to be taken from them. Chapter 6 explores implications for leadership, in general, and then explores implications for the administration of educational systems, in particular. The epilogue provides some closure, but also gives room for future dialogue and work.

Each chapter of the book begins with the continuing story of Leslie O'Connor, principal of Washington School. The fictional story follows Leslie as she struggles with her leadership role as a building administrator. Chapter 1 begins by introducing Leslie and how she struggles with her classical management training and experience. Each subsequent chapter weaves the experiences of Leslie as she learns more about these new leadership ideas and how they affect her job. In this way, the reader gets to see how a building leader can apply these new lessons on the job—in an entertaining fashion. (The theme for the narrative about Leslie was created by Rettig [2000].)

Each chapter concludes with a number of questions in "Points to Ponder" that may help to focus the reader's attention to the important points presented in the chapter. This portion of the chapter includes analysis and application questions for readers to be able to use in their own settings.

Before proceeding with this text, it would be very beneficial to understand the author's use of some key terminology. Various people define the following critical words quite differently, so it would be appropriate to understand how they are used subsequently.

Leadership—Leadership is considered the ability to move others toward a vision. This can be the leader's vision, or it can refer to the defining and integration of a community vision—as will be used in this book. Leadership is to be considered in a broader context than administration or management. Management implies maintaining the status quo, while leadership implies creating change.

Administration—In this book, administration refers to the administration of responsibilities associated with the duties of management. In other words, here, administration refers to more typical management functions and could be used interchangeably with the term, "management."

Newtonian Physics—Newtonian physics is also referred to as traditional and classical physics. This is a science of hypothesis formulation, deduction, and testing. It is a very controlled science whereby the observer is detached from the observed. It is a study of the parts in order to understand the whole. Much of Sir Isaac Newton's work was based on the principles developed by the likes of Copernicus, Ptolemy, Kepler, and Galileo. But it was Newton who developed the complete and substantial theoretical body that became the foundation for today's classical physics.

Quantum Physics—While there is a minor difference in definition, in many cases, the terms quantum physics and quantum mechanics are used interchangeably. Here, it is the study of the behavior of subatomic particles and describes various outcomes as statistical potentials or probabilities.

Newer Sciences—While none of these newer sciences are actually all that new, their study and application by the general public is very recent. For example, quantum physics has been a science for about one hundred years, but most people know very little about it. For the purpose of this book, the primary descriptions of the newer sciences would include: chaos theory, the science of complexity, fractals, fields theories, dissipative structures, and chemical clocks. A secondary focus will include biological and ecological systems, the study of weather, and even economics.

Newtonian Model of Leadership—The Newtonian model (or approach) focuses on the work of the administrator. The vision belongs to the administrator who uses such traditional techniques of coercion, manipulation, control, efficiency, impersonal orientation, and a rigid hierarchy to implement this vision. In its purest sense, the author uses the terms "Newtonian model" and "Authoritarian model" interchangeably, because that is the practice toward which most current administrators lean.

Quantum Model of Leadership—The literature has not defined a quantum model of leadership per se. The quantum model of leadership is really being defined here for the first time. This is a model that reasserts the human equation in leadership by focusing on dynamic relationships, communication, and systems thinking. Here, leadership comes from all parts of the system.

Reductionism—In this text, reductionism refers to an approach—both scientific and the process of studying systems—of viewing things in ever smaller parts. It is the view that something is equal to the sum of its parts. This procedure is aimed at isolating parts to study them, analyze them, and then put them back together.

Behaviorism—Behaviorism is considered the objective study of behavior that results in quantifiably measurable data. In terms of pedagogy, it refers to teacher-centered instruction where learning is broken down into incremental skill parts or units. In terms of leadership, behaviorism reflects the typical management style used in most organizations today.

Systems Thinking—Systems thinking is a way of understanding a system or an organization "in terms of connectedness, relationships, [and] context" (Capra, 1996, p. 29). The whole is more than the sum of the parts. One can only understand an organization by studying the whole organization over time and space, not in isolated pieces.

While this book does cover issues and concepts relevant to leadership in general, its primary focus will be confined to that of educational leadership. Furthermore, you might be concerned by your lack of knowledge in these sciences. Often experts are not the ones who come up with great insights, however. In other words, you don't have to understand the science. Perhaps the lay person is the one who can make the greatest difference. In the words of chaos theorist James Gleick (1987, p. 37), "There are two revolutions. A new science arises out of one that has reached a dead end. Often a revolution has an interdisciplinary character—its central discoveries often come from people straying outside the normal bounds of their specialties." Hopefully, by the time you finish this book, you will have a better understanding of how our educational leadership training has been wrong, you'll have a new model for your own leadership, and you will have ideas for both short-term and long-term change in your own system.

The Newtonian Approach to Leadership

> If the mind is brightened and your wisdom purified, then one hair and all the universe can be interfused, for there is nothing that is outside the mind. . . . The wisdom of the tathagatas is just like this: it is complete in the bodies of all sentient beings. Merely ordinary, foolish people do not recognize it.
>
> —Korean philosopher Chinul (cited by Shim in McGreal, 1995, p. 408)

LESLIE'S LAMENT

On the outskirts of the busy city of Britton sits Washington School. Built in 1961, Washington has been through many changes in student demographics, programs offered for its changing student population, and curricular adaptations to meet changing philosophies of pedagogy and student expectations. On this sunny October Friday afternoon, Principal Leslie O'Connor looks out of her office window and tries to make sense of this eclectic menagerie of students, curriculum, and activities.

Leslie had graduated from a small private college with a degree in English education. She truly believed that her liberal arts education prepared her quite well to work with today's students. Upon graduation, she already had a teaching job lined up. Indeed, her college education did help her in working with all kinds of people, yet she felt woefully inadequate in terms of writing curriculum and the pedagogy necessary to teach these children. She considered this simply to be the way things were. *Most of our learning comes from on-the-job training after all*, she thought to herself. Still, she cursed her college for not preparing her for the real world.

Because she had taken on a variety of leadership roles throughout her life, Leslie knew it would be only a matter of time before she became a leader in education. The principalship seemed only appropriate for her. So, after a one-semester break from college classes, Leslie enrolled in an educational leadership master's degree program at the nearby urban university. Leslie was on the fast track to school leadership. She was making all the right moves, and her colleagues always told her that she would be their boss some day. Leslie smiled with a modicum of humility. She liked the idea of being the boss, but at the same time she knew how important the role would be. She took her studies seriously.

Still, Leslie had an unsettling feeling in her stomach as she sat in those graduate courses and as she read *those* textbooks. While she enjoyed reading and learning about the important figures and their theories of educational administration, she felt all the approaches were too simple, too much like recipes. Over and over she heard the subliminal message that the administrator was the boss, how he or she should go about making decisions, and how he or she should plan. Intuitively, she felt these approaches were cold, calculated, and created separation among the people. These approaches seemed too analytical. They did not jibe with what she knew about people and how complex social systems and organizations actually behaved. Leslie O'Connor wasn't sure she wanted to work in this kind of world. Leslie graduated from her program with an A/B grade-point average. She had done everything right and had the support of everyone.

In the spring of her graduation, Leslie had four interviews for principalships—she was offered three of them. Leslie decided on Britton because the city was very similar in size and demographics to the town in which she grew up and was only two hours away from her parents' home. She left her teaching job, her friends, and her familiar apartment with a great deal of trepidation, but a healthy amount of excitement. Over the next year, she would lose a sense of both.

THE SCIENCE

Our current notions of leadership are thoroughly based on the science of Newtonian physics. The traditional or classical models expect a great deal of control and authority by those in leadership positions. Newtonian physics has helped man to understand the movement of the planets in our solar system and of the stars in the heavens. It has helped man create machines that operate with expected and planned efficiency. It has provided man with comforts and luxuries that have helped to make life more livable and even enjoyable. This has been a good science for so much of what we need and use today. It has helped to create an existence of mechanistic simplicity. But the science is flawed when it comes to understanding the lives of people and of the phenomenon of work environments. Newtonian science is linear and perhaps is sufficient for the understanding of machines, but not for the understanding of the complexities of living creatures, humans, and their social organizations.

Classical physics seemed to provide the opportunity for scientists to better understand *things*. As the science explicitly suggests, if you can just break down the complex whole and study its parts individually, you can understand the whole and make predictions about its future. You can then provide an algorithm for success and for replication. This philosophy might work for machines and planetary movements, but it cannot do justice to understanding the complexities of people and of the organizations within which they work and live. This traditional approach is appropriate for its area of study—closed, mechanical systems. Unfortunately, scientists and theorists in other fields have taken its fundamental principles and applied them to fields that don't fit the approach. For example, behaviorists like John Watson and B. F. Skinner applied this Newtonian physics of mechanistic linear prediction to the study of human life and behavior. "Economists, philosophers, and political theorists soon grafted Newton's natural law onto all aspects of life. The late eighteenth century's Enlightenment, a culmination of triumphs for the left hemisphere, celebrated in advance the inevitable taming of both wild nature and irrational behavior" (Shlain, 1998, p. 378). However, the science is inappropriate here. Physics professor at the University of California at Berkeley Henry Stapp (1993) posited:

> The behaviorists sought to explain human behavior in terms of certain relatively simple mechanisms, such as stimulus and response, habit formation, habit integration, and conditioning of various kinds. It is now generally agreed that the simple mechanisms identified by the behaviorists cannot adequately account for the full complexities of human behavior. (p. 13)

Frederick Taylor then applied this same method to understanding how to make employees work more efficiently and how to provide the leadership to control the desired results. Stephen Covey explained his concern with this line of reasoning. "You simply can't think *efficiency* with people. You think *effectiveness* with *people* and *efficiency* with *things*" (1990, p. 169). The flaw lies in the belief that people can be dissected and understood and controlled like machines. It believes that leaders must motivate and think for the workers. It believes that work must be broken down into ever smaller parts in order to understand the whole. It does not take into account the human equation. It does not take into account how the parts affect the whole in interconnected ways that cannot be measured in isolation. It does not take into account the incomprehensible interconnectedness of the relationships within the whole. It does not fit the study of humans and their organizations. Margaret Wheatley (1994a), a former professor of management at Brigham Young University and a leading thinker in the new sciences, perhaps summarizes this discussion best:

> Each of us lives and works in organizations designed from Newtonian images of the universe. We manage by separating things into parts, we believe that influence occurs as a direct result of force exerted from one person to another, we engage in complex planning for a world that we keep expecting to be predictable, and we search continually for better methods of objectively perceiving the world. . . . [These assumptions] are the base from which we design and manage organizations, and from which we do research in all of the social sciences. Intentionally or not, we work from a world view that has been derived from natural sciences. (p. 6)

In order to see why this traditional approach to leadership based upon classical physics is inappropriate, it is necessary to understand the physics. The next section will briefly describe the key principles of classical physics, which will be followed by a brief description of the key principles of classical leadership.

KEY PRINCIPLES OF CLASSICAL PHYSICS

Classical physics starts with the premise that objectivity leads to predictability. In order to make predictions, the researcher must be completely objective; there must be a separation of the subject and the object. In other words, the observer must not be part of the experiment—they must look in from the outside. Robert Palter (1970, p. 244) explained the

Newtonian "hypothetico-deductive method" as encompassing three critical parts: formulation, deduction, and testing. The observer needs to control the experiment, manipulate the variables, and observe the changes. Each variable (in theory) can be quantified through this process; every conceivable variable can be given a numerical value and placed into a formula. By isolating the variables, the observer can then replicate the experiment, seek consistency, and ultimately seek predictability. According to theoretical physicist and former professor at San Diego State University and the University of Paris Fred Alan Wolf (1988),

> there are three laws [of classical physics] as conceived by Sir Isaac Newton: (1) A body in motion tends to stay in motion—the principle of inertia. (2) A force acting on a body will cause that body to accelerate—either speed up, slow down, or change its direction through space. (3) A force acting on a body will cause that body to return an equal and oppositely directed force on the source of the original force. (p. 322)

It's quite apparent that classical physics is founded on linear, mechanistic thinking. The foundation of this science is a study of the parts in a reductionistic way of looking at things. The notion of things is so very important to classical physics. This physics has the aim of reducing the whole into ever smaller parts. The idea is that if we can break the whole into small enough parts, we can study those parts individually, and then put them back together to better understand the whole. This might be relatively easy with closed systems such as machines. Each component is taken apart, studied in detail, and put back together. This can be done with things. For the purposes here, the key principles of classical physics are:

(1) reductionism
(2) objectivity
(3) control
(4) replication
(5) prediction

Unfortunately, this method is inappropriate beyond its limited uses. As systems thinker Peter Senge (1990) put it,

> From a very early age, we are taught to break apart problems, to fragment the world. This apparently makes complex tasks and subjects more

manageable, but we pay a hidden, enormous price. We can no longer see the consequences of our actions; we lose our intrinsic sense of connection to a larger whole. (p. 3)

Just how do these principles of Newtonian physics impact our notions of leadership? The following section will describe the concepts from classical physics that administrators have borrowed to create our traditional models of leadership.

KEY PRINCIPLES OF CLASSICAL LEADERSHIP

It must be made clear that there is not an explicit Newtonian *model* of leadership; however, it is this author's assertion that traditional models of leadership have built their foundations upon the principles of classical physics. For example, the science of behaviorism came from the thinking of classical physics. "In reaction to the subjectivity inherent in introspection, behaviorists held that the scientific study of psychology must restrict itself to the study of observable behaviors and the stimulus conditions that control them" (Bransford, Brown, & Cocking, 1999, p. 6). Behaviorism is defined as the objective study of measurable behaviors, rather than a focus on mental processes. The observer is expected to step back from the experiment in an analytical posture, to control the experiment, to isolate and manipulate the variables, and then to predict the future. Behaviorism, as developed by John B. Watson and B. F. Skinner, uses the characteristic techniques of stimulus-response and conditioning to observe changes in the person or animal. Here, people and animals, and even systems, are viewed as things. "To Watson, people were like simple adding machines" (McConnell, 1980, p. 142). Still, behaviorism leaves no room for creativity, thinking, problem solving, and emotions; it does not leave room for much of what is uniquely human.

The management model of classical organizational thought, also referred to as scientific management, has its roots in Newtonian physics, too. Actually, scientific management was the model of leadership just prior to the work of Watson and Skinner, yet reflected the thinking of the time. Nevertheless, this model uses a machine metaphor to view and direct workers and the systems in which they work. The purpose was to provide efficient labor, and the work of Frederick Taylor epitomized this thinking. In this regard, time and motion studies were conducted in order to organize each type of work so that time and effort were minimized. Basic features of this model are well known to all who have studied leadership. In order to provide for routine performance, there is a standardization of tasks. Through division of labor there is a specialization of tasks and an impersonal hierarchy. (While there is a specialization of tasks, they become standardized within their specialization.)

This impersonal hierarchy is established through a pyramid model where the optimal number of people under any one person's span of control should be five to ten workers. There is also a uniqueness of function where each department does its own work and there is no duplication of work by other departments. Finally, there is always identification of the formal organization as can be viewed by the organizational blueprint or flowchart of hierarchy and responsibility. To explicate this practice, Wayne Hoy and Cecil Miskel (1982, p. 10) wrote, "[Early students of educational administration] observed administrators at work, specifying the component tasks to be performed, determining more effective ways to perform each task, and suggesting an organization to maximize efficiency." Systems expert Peter Block (1996, p. 101) saw this management thought process when he wrote, "Functional organizations, with deep silos, are the ideal structure for command-and-control governance. They were born of the industrial revolution where economies of scale and specialization of labor became the religion." In 1999, the National Research Council wrote (Bransford, Brown, & Cocking, 1999),

> School administrators were eager to make use of the "scientific" organization of factories to structure efficient classrooms. Children were regarded as raw materials to be efficiently processed by technical workers (the teachers) to reach the end product. . . . Teachers were viewed as workers whose job was to carry out directives from their superiors—the efficiency experts of schooling (administrators and researchers). (p. 120)

Classical organization management was the model of practice from 1900 to 1930. Two other major models or approaches have attempted to improve on its shortcomings. From 1930 to 1950 the "people-oriented" human relations approach took over as a reaction to classical organizational management's failure to acknowledge the informal organization, the intrinsic motivation of the workers, the dynamics of social systems, and the idiosyncrasies of the individual. The now famous Western Electric Hawthorne Studies (Hoy & Miskel, 1982) showed:

(1) The economic incentive is not the only significant motivator. In fact, noneconomic social sanctions limit the effectiveness of economic incentives.

(2) Workers respond to management as members of an informal group, not as individuals.

(3) Production levels are limited more by the social norms of the informal organization than by physiological capacities.

(4) Specialization does not necessarily create the most efficient organization of the work group.

(5) Workers use the informal organization to protect themselves against arbitrary management decisions.

(6) Informal social organizations will interact with management.

(7) A narrow span of control is not a prerequisite to effective supervision.

(8) Informal leaders are often as important as formal supervisors.

(9) Individuals are active human beings, not passive cogs in a machine. (pp. 8–9)

Jean Lipman-Blumen—a management expert—(1996, p. 62) further stated that, "It soon became apparent that the small group—not just managerial authority—was an important source of workers' commitment and discipline." She went on to explain, "When people participate in the decision making process, they tend to become more committed to the decision and therefore more likely willing to implement it" (p. 62).

Many organizational managers felt that the human relations approach did not provide accountability and was too laissez-faire in practice. So while behaviorism was in its prime, the behavioral science model was born in 1950. Chester I. Barnard pioneered much of this work. Hoy and Miskel described the change in focus. "Democratic prescription was replaced by analysis, a field orientation by a discipline orientation, raw observation by theoretical research" (1982, p. 11). Still, no matter the pervading thought of the time, much of the classical organization thought has existed and continues to exist, to varying degrees, in current administrative practices, as is discussed later in this chapter.

Douglas McGregor (1960) developed a seminal work in the study of management with his description of Theory X and Theory Y. Theory X managers follow the more classical physics approach of supervising employees, where Theory Y managers deal more in the relational realm of administration. The basic features of Theory X include:

(1) Average people are by nature indolent—they work as little as possible.

(2) They lack ambition, dislike responsibility, prefer to be led.

(3) They are inherently self-centered, indifferent to organizational needs.

(4) They are by nature resistant to change.

(5) They are gullible, not very bright, ready dupes of the charlatan and demagogue. (Douglas McGregor cited in Sergiovanni & Starratt, 1993, p. 15).

The basic features of Theory Y include:

(1) Management is responsible for organizing the elements of production enterprise—money, materials, equipment, people—in the interest of economic (educational) ends.

(2) People are *not* [emphasis in original] by nature passive or resistant to organizational needs. They have become so as a result of experience in organizations.

(3) The motivation, the potential for development, the capacity for assuming responsibility, the readiness to direct behaviors toward organizational goals are all present in people; management does not put them there. It is a responsibility of management to make it all possible for people to recognize and develop these human characteristics for themselves.

(4) The essential task of management is to arrange organizational conditions and methods of operation so that people can achieve their own goals *best* (emphasis in original) by directing *their* (emphasis in original) own efforts toward organizational objectives. (McGregor cited in Sergiovanni & Starratt, 1993, p. 16)

As was mentioned earlier, other models of leadership with various names have been initiated since the advent of classical scientific management; none typically is practiced in its purest theoretical form. However, the traditional model of leadership maintains a stronghold in many of today's current administrative practices. Before reading further in this book, the reader is reminded that the original premise here must be clear; Newtonian physics is the foundation of the classical organizational leadership approach and the behavioral science approach, and these approaches remain entrenched in leadership behavior, today.

VESTIGES OF THE CLASSICAL LEADERSHIP
AND ADMINISTRATION MODELS

Few administrators would consider themselves of the "old school." They feel they take into account the informal organization and treat people like people. To varying degrees, they are correct. In other words, most administrators are more eclectic in style and are more likely to practice situational leadership. Still, much of their practice is more classical than they might want to admit, even in these times of site-based management, peer supervision, and professional associations. To give a flavor of these remnants of classical organizational thought, and without belaboring the point, the remainder of this chapter focuses on only a few key areas of educational systems: organizational structure and communication, supervision and evaluation of staff, curriculum and instruction, and budgeting.

ORGANIZATIONAL STRUCTURE AND COMMUNICATION

Our leaders work within systems that are highly, and rigidly, structured. The hierarchy is a top-down model wherein different silos (departments and subject areas) are aligned for efficiency and standardization. Most medium- and larger-sized school districts have a superintendent at the top of the hierarchy. Directly under them are either deputies, or directors, or assistant superintendents who have people in specialized areas reporting to them. For example, there quite likely is a director of personnel, a director of pupil services, a director of business services, and a director of curriculum and instruction. Each of these directors will supervise five to ten people with more specialized roles and expertise. While the personnel function might be the exception to the rule with only one or two specialized individuals, the other areas prove this point. The director of pupil services could well supervise professional staff with specialization in learning disabilities, emotional/behavioral disabilities, cognitive disabilities, and an enormous variety of physical disabilities. School psychologists and social workers might also report to the director of pupil services. In cases where several people work within a subspecialized area, coordinators might be assigned to them. For example, a district that employs six or more school psychologists and six or more social workers could well have coordinators for both of these specialties.

The director of business services will directly supervise a controller (interesting title for a manager), an MIS manager, a coordinator of purchasing and shipping, a coordinator of food services, and a coordinator of buildings and grounds. Again, each of these coordinators may have other administrators working under his or her supervision. The director of curriculum and instruction will most likely have coordinators in the areas of reading and language arts, foreign languages, mathematics and science, social sciences, ESL/bilingual, art, music, physical education and health, and perhaps research and development.

Each of these major function areas (personnel, business services, pupil services, and curriculum and instruction) has its own systems of accountability and bureaucracy. Tedious and microscopic budgeting processes provide accountability for business services, while personnel services use very prescriptive collective bargaining agreements. Pupil services is clearly governed by federal and state laws that detail how students, teachers, and programs are identified, serviced, and evaluated.

Curriculum and instruction has numerous committees that must proceed through various levels of permission for curriculum changes and textbook adoption. Student and curriculum evaluation are the hallmark of accountability in this function area. The entire organization is governed by hundreds of impersonal policies that are developed and passed by the administration and the board of education. Communication is clearly funneled through hierarchical flow charts. E-mail and memoranda rule the day. Command, control, replication—this blueprint is found everywhere across the country.

Even individual school sites are structured systems within a larger system. There is a principal at the top of the hierarchy with various assistants and coordinators reporting to him or her. Both administrators and teachers alike follow the same policies and procedures as the centralized workers outlined above.

SUPERVISION AND EVALUATION OF STAFF

The superintendent is responsible for providing supervision and evaluation of the directors who in turn are responsible for the supervision and evaluation of their coordinators. Either the superintendent or assistants are also responsible for providing supervision and evaluation of building principals. Likewise, the principals then are expected to provide clinical supervision and evaluation of teachers, as well as for classified staff—right down the hierarchy.

Sadly, teachers often complain that the supervision that they receive is more perfunctory in nature and meaningless to them (Rettig, 1999). They are observed very infrequently and then receive a written report as to the effectiveness of their work. The summative evaluations at the end of the year are typically based upon these infrequent observation reports. These observation and evaluation forms are very detailed in what is expected of the teacher and in the levels of performance. Each teacher is rated using the same forms. Individualized supervision and evaluation are the exception, not the rule. Forms are "in," personal plans are cursory, at best. It's as if quality teaching can be captured on a checklist and replicated to all settings. Consistency, control, and standardization are valued as desirable.

CURRICULUM/INSTRUCTION AND ASSESSMENT

The National Research Council stipulated, "The factory model affect[s] the design of curriculum, instruction, and assessment in schools" (Bransford, et al., 1999, p. 120). Teachers are typically not allowed to unilaterally choose their own textbooks and curriculum. They usually must follow the prescribed curriculum guide provided by the school district. There is renewed interest in state and national curricula. Likewise, they must use textbooks that have been written by external publishers and adopted by the board of education. There is an emphasis on consistency and standardization. Many of these textbooks attempt to "teacher proof" the job of educators. Furthermore, there is an increasing emphasis at both the local and state levels for standardization of assessment and testing of students. In other words, the curriculum, the instruction, and the assessment tools are becoming more and more homogeneous and similar from school to school. There is an increasing desire to make each school look alike. In a chilling review of the path American education has followed, Noam Chomsky (2000) warned:

> Schools [are] institutions for indoctrination and for imposing obedience. Far from creating independent thinkers, schools have always, throughout history, played an institutional role in a system of control and coercion. And once you are well educated, you have already been socialized in ways that support the power structure, which in turn rewards you immensely. (p. 16)

BUDGETING

School district budgets are most often highly centralized. State standardized accounting systems are mandated. Clearly, the process is extremely structured. The largest expenditure of each district budget—staff salaries and benefits—is under the control of the centralized office of personnel. The next largest district expenditures, facilities management and technology, are typically under the control of the centralized office of business services. Schools are allocated a per-pupil amount that usually falls somewhere around $100. At the building level, principals often decide how much money is allotted to each teacher, program, or department. With this money teachers are expected to buy supplies and supplemental materials for their instruction. Ultimately, very little money is directly provided to the teachers—those people who work most closely with the students. The budgeting process expects consistency, control, and standardization. While good arguments can be made that school system budgets are things that can and should follow linear lessons from the classical sciences, the point here is not to change current accounting practices. Rather, the point is that more emphasis should be given to the local level for budgeting decisions.

While other important areas of educational systems (student discipline, staff motivation, pay systems, hiring practices, etc.) could have been chosen to be critiqued here, the above areas are perhaps most crucial and integral to education. Without going into too much detail, it would appear evident that much of the leadership that occurs in schools and school systems remains deeply entrenched in the lessons learned from classical physics. To reiterate what was mentioned earlier in the chapter, the key features of classical physics are reductionism, objectivity, control, replication, and prediction. Each one of these elements is clearly visible in the ways that school systems are organized and administered. Vaclav Havel, famous author and former president of the Czech Republic, offers a fitting conclusion to this chapter (cited in Bolman & Deal, 1995):

> Classical modern science described only the surface of things, a single dimension of reality. And the more dogmatically science treated it as the only dimension, as the very essence of reality, the more misleading it became. We may know immeasurably more about the universe than our ancestors did, and yet it increasingly seems they knew something more essential about it than we do; something that escapes us. (p. 7)

POINTS TO PONDER

1. How is Leslie's setting similar to your setting?
2. What types of concerns does Leslie have that you share?
3. What are the characteristics of traditional organizations?
4. What are the strengths of traditional organizations? Why?
5. What are the limitations of traditional organizations? Why?
6. With which assertions in this chapter do you agree?
7. With which assertions in this chapter do you disagree? Why?
8. Can you describe other areas in which school systems are clearly classical?

CHAPTER 2

The Model Does Not Fit and It Never Did

While some parts of the universe may operate like machines, these are closed systems, and closed systems, at best, form only a small part of the physical universe. Most phenomenon of interest to us are, in fact, open systems, exchanging energy or matter (and, one might add, information) with their environment. Surely biological and social systems are open, which means that the attempt to understand them in mechanistic terms is doomed to failure. This suggests, moreover, that most of reality, instead of being orderly, stable, and equilibrial, is seething and bubbling with change, disorder, and process.

— Alvin Toffler (cited in Prigogine & Stengers, 1984, p. xv)

LESLIE'S LAMENT

Leslie loved meeting the staff, the teachers, and her new administrator colleagues. Still, she remembered back to her first year of teaching and how she felt about not being adequately prepared for teaching. Now she felt even worse. She was too young for this responsibility. She should have taken an assistant principalship first. She didn't know any of the answers; heck, she hardly knew the questions. That was the issue, she thought. "The worst part of this job is not knowing what is expected of me and what has to be done next."

Leslie did feel lucky, though. She had two excellent secretaries who had been at Washington School for fifteen and twelve years. Indeed, that made a huge difference. To her great surprise, Leslie spent nearly all her time in August doing managerial kinds of things. She had to learn the budget, make certain all materials and supplies had arrived, and she had to keep maintenance projects on schedule. This took too much of her time, but she had no choice. She was really worried that she did not know enough about the curricula and assessment requirements for this district. How could she have intelligent conversations about the curriculum with parents, teachers, and board members if she really didn't know these answers? She made up her mind to immerse herself in these topics.

Leslie did find part of the job enjoyable and compelling. She loved to interview new teacher and classified staff candidates. While she exhausted after a full day of interviewing, she always felt that this would be the most important part of her job. She needed to surround herself with quality people—people who would build a caring community for kids. She also loved to visit with her secretaries and the custodial staff. They took some lunches and breaks together in August. These people would be very important to her. In fact, one afternoon Leslie changed into her old sweats so she could assist the head custodian in waxing and buffing the hall floors. She avoided the gymnasium as the lacquer smell made her nauseous.

So, Leslie sat on her desk on this sunny October morning looking out her window. This job really wasn't what she thought it would be. She definitely felt like the boss, but not much of a leader. She spent all her time making decisions, yet whom or what did she lead? *Perhaps this leadership thing is really ethereal*, she thought out loud. Flushed by embarrassment for talking out loud to herself, Leslie got up and went outside for a walk around the playground. She had to clear her mind.

Leslie enjoyed these solitary walks around the campus. They gave her the opportunity to clear her head. They seemed like her only time to stop and smell the roses, albeit roses painted on a mural on the exterior gym walls. In one sense, she was pretty happy with herself. With the exception of the occasional parent complaint about getting the wrong teacher, too much homework, not enough homework, or teacher complaint about cafeteria duty, things were going pretty smoothly. Leslie knew she could leave the school for a day or two and everything would run as expected. On the other hand, that was part of the problem. To a large extent, it didn't seem to matter what Leslie did—she didn't seem to be in control. From her experience as a teacher, and from her graduate studies, she believed that the principal was always in control. Perhaps this was more a facade. On second thought, it was more likely that this uneasy feeling was coming from a lack of administrative experience. Certainly she'd have things more under control in a couple of years. Suddenly, she was shocked out of her deep thought by the clashing school bell. Time to get back to work!

Leslie arrived at work at 7:15 on Monday morning. She wanted to spend some time looking over the business director's proposal to realign the organization of the central office technology staff. Leslie wasn't sure that any changes would have any impact on her school. "Why would they?" At 7:33 Leslie was interrupted from her analysis—Mrs. Faulke stopped in to discuss her concerns regarding her daughter's field trip to see the art museum. It seemed that some of the artwork was of questionable taste. Leslie was torn between the need to support the autonomy of the teachers to plan such a trip and the rights of the parents to express their legitimate concerns. Leslie wished the teachers would be more aware of these concerns, and she also wished that parents went to the teachers to express their concerns. By the time Leslie finished her discussion with Mrs. Faulke, the bell announced the beginning of another day. The sense of a lack of control began to creep in again.

After the teachers and students were back in their classrooms from their lunch hour, Leslie found herself back in her more and more familiar place—sitting upon her desk looking out the window.

"Do we know what we're doing here?" she questioned herself in silence. "How can I provide leadership to these teachers when we don't seem to have any true understanding of our purpose, and much less any idea of how to get there?"

Leslie decided to call her older sister, a marketing executive, just to talk. Cindy was always there to lend an ear when Leslie became frustrated. The phone calls were becoming more numerous this past year.

Leslie began, "Hi, Cindy. It's me, again. Any big contracts today?"

"Same old, same ol'," Cindy responded. "What's up now? No, let me guess. A parent is complaining that too much time is spent using computers and not enough time on the basics. No, no. Teachers are in the lounge complaining that the new state standardized tests don't measure the higher-level thinking skills that must be taught. No, I know. The superintendent has initiated a new model of principal evaluations based on student outcomes. That's it, right?"

After a long pause, Leslie sullenly answered, "I don't know. I don't know what I'm doing here. I want to feel we're doing something significant here, but it seems like we're going through the motions. I just don't know."

Cindy had learned over the years to not give much advice. It was better to just listen and let Leslie think out loud and come to her own conclusions. So her response was a simple, "You and me both."

"What do you mean, 'You and me both'?" I went into education so that I could do something important for people, not to make money!"

Cindy had to break her vow of silence. "Listen, Ms. Martyr! You make decent money, and educators are not in an exclusive club of people who help others. Lord help me; I might get to heaven some day, too!"

"I didn't mean that . . . "

"Listen, teachers always think that they are underpaid and unappreciated. They think they are the only ones who work to help others. They think that nobody understands them. They think . . ."

"Okay, okay, Cindy. You've made your point."

"No, I haven't Leslie," Cindy retorted. Trying to calm herself, she hesitated, "I think teachers, by and large, probably are underappreciated. Still, their pay and benefits are reasonable. On the other hand, they did go into education to help others, to work with children. They should not be penalized for that, but the point I want to make is that they are not the only ones who work to help others. All of society benefits from the work we all do as a community. We each play an important role, and few of us get paid what we feel is fair."

Leslie had recovered from her sister's diatribe and decided to get to the real issue. "I'm concerned that I don't know what is going on in my own building. I go from one mini-crisis to another, from one meeting to another, from one in-service to another, from one teacher observation to another, and I'm not sure that anything I do makes a difference. I feel out of control, or at least that I don't control anything. There are these two educational theorists that I read about, Lee Bolman and Terrence Deal, who believe that schools are loosely coupled systems. They feel that all the things we do go on in isolation with little connection, and yet we put on airs of rational, organized structure and cohesion."

"All jobs are like that, Leslie," was Cindy's reply. "I have held several different jobs over the years and work with many different companies today. They are all loosely coupled systems. They make poor decisions, decisions are often made on emotion, huge amounts of money are spent at times without a great deal of thought, and there is little participatory management, as they would have you believe. None of our systems are as cohesive and rational as we might like to think, or as we portray to our larger publics."

"Really? You mean you have workers who gossip and complain? You have bosses who make decisions that are not based upon the data you provide them? You mean they waste money? You mean one department doesn't know what the other is doing?" questioned Leslie, hoping that she was not alone.

"Well, yes and no," came Cindy's response. "Nothing is always that way. We continually try to make rational decisions and watch our budgets. That is extremely important to us. But we don't always make the best decisions. We adopt new ideas in the hope that they will work. People do complain and waste time, but they also work hard and care about their jobs. I guess this is what it's about when people work together in any organization."

"Okay! So all organizations are far from perfect. What can I as a leader do to get a hold of this imperfect system? How can I get it under control?"

Cindy exclaimed, "That's the problem. You can't get hold of it. You can't control it. These human work systems are like . . . like an ecological system, I guess. In an ecological system, nothing controls anything. Still, because everything is interconnected, they do impact each other. Don't try to control, let the system work naturally."

"Then why have a principal? Why have a leader? Ecological systems don't have administrators!" exclaimed Leslie in exasperation.

"You're right, of course," Cindy said. "Perhaps we must redefine leadership. But listen, I have to go meet with a client. Let's have lunch at your place on Saturday. I'll bring Chinese. In the meantime, let's both reflect on this ecological system stuff. Is that a good metaphor? How can leadership be redefined?"

"All right, but I had hoped for a better answer from you when I called," Leslie muttered. She looked at her calendar. She had to be in Mary Thompson's science classroom for an observation in ten minutes.

Mary Thompson, a veteran teacher of twenty-eight years, had won the district "Teacher of the Year" award twice in the past ten years. She had written much of the innovative curriculum that the science teachers throughout the district used. She was also on the board of the state science teachers association. Mary Thompson was a master teacher, and the parents knew it. Numerous parent requests for her classroom made it quite difficult for the principal to schedule heterogeneous classes each year.

Leslie sat at Mary's desk while observing her introduce the science lesson to her youthful charges. Leslie glanced at her notes to remind herself of their preconference. With all Mary's experience and expertise, she still got nervous when being observed by the principal. Undoubtedly, that was why Mary asked Leslie to observe her introductory science class—part of her comfort zone. Leslie knew it would be a successful lesson, but would she be able to help Mary grow professionally?

"Why am I here?" Leslie whispered to herself—one of the boys looked at Leslie in confusion. "I'm probably a thorn in Mary's side, and I don't know what good advice I would possibly be able to give her—something that she has never heard before. Who am I to give Mary Thompson advice?"

The lesson blurred in front of Leslie as she sat writing all the components of a good lesson. Mary was clearly a pro. Leslie found herself drifting to the conversation she just had with Cindy.

I wonder how Cindy is evaluated? Leslie daydreamed. *Does she get observed? How does she evaluate her employees? Does she observe them?* In her pocket calendar, Leslie wrote these questions to ask Cindy when she saw her on Saturday.

Mary continued with her lesson. She finished on time, the kids enjoyed it, and it was clear that they learned a little something along the way.

Leslie went back to her office to analyze her notes and to try to come up with something profound to tell Mary. But she immediately found a message waiting from the superintendent. One activity and small crisis after another filled her day until she noticed it was already 5:02—time to go home. Leslie resigned herself to finishing Mary's observation report this coming weekend.

THE SCIENCE

One can look at two fundamental reasons why Newtonian physics should not serve as an approach for leadership models. The primary reason is that it is an inappropriate way to treat and to work with people. Classical science has debased nature. We have made nature a thing of our control—something we can analyze with our crude instruments. No matter how much the behaviorists wish for the efficiency of stimulus and response, people are not robots. The secondary reason that classical physics should not serve as an approach to leadership models is that organizations are not black and white, and they do not fit precisely into algorithms.

CLASSICAL SCIENCE NOT APPROPRIATE
FOR THE STUDY OF PEOPLE

People are not machines. They can't be viewed in terms of variables and efficiency coefficients. People are very diverse and dynamic. They have values, emotions, feelings, and personal motivations. To treat them any other way is immoral. To be in a position of power is to be in a position of moral obligation. "The obligation of accepting a position of power is to be, above all else, a good human being" (Block, 1996, p. 42). In a concurring statement, educational leadership expert Thomas Sergiovanni (1990) wrote:

> In value-added leadership authority takes on moral characteristics. . . . Whenever there is an unequal distribution of power between two people, the relationship becomes a moral one. Leadership involves an offer to control. The follower accepts this offer on the assumption that control will not be exploited. In this sense leadership is not a right but a responsibility. (p. 28)

In the traditional authoritarian workplace, the employee is seen as a means to an end. "Seen simply as 'factors of production,' employees were *not* [emphasis in original] expected to have opinions about how to do things, much less how to do things better" (Lipman-Blumen, 1996, p. 58). While such bureaucratic heavy-handedness promoted efficiency at the surface, its negative features were noticeably worse. As Jean Lipman-Blumen (1996, p. 61) posited, "Eventually, the self-defeating effects of naked authoritarianism became evident in sagging morale, skyrocketing turnover, worker sabotage, costly strikes, and low-quality products."

Humans are part of nature, not apart from nature. Classical science has debased nature, and thus has debased mankind. Japanese philosopher Nishitani Keiji believed,

> Science as understood in the age of modernity, involves an objectification not only of the natural world, but likewise of the human subject itself, and thereby results in the depersonalization of nature. Such a situation leads to an . . . almost worship-like attitude with which moderns regard science. (cited in Habito, 1995, p. 396)

Again, the message should be clear. Classical physics is the science appropriate for the study of things, not the study of people. Systems thinker Joseph Jaworski interviewed quantum physicist David Bohm. In the interview, Bohm stated, "This is a paradox. You cannot understand it [the human world] if you try to use classical thinking as a standard" (Jaworski, 1996, p. 176). Newtonian physics does not have the language needed to understand the human equation.

Interestingly, it is no longer the scientists who are making these mistakes. Scientists understand that the classical science is inappropriate for the study of people. It's the educational and organizational practitioners who are in error. In a most intriguing insight, Margaret Wheatley (1994a) quipped:

> We social scientists are trying hard to be conscientious, using the methodologies and thought patterns of seventeenth-century science, while the scientists, traveling away from us at the speed of light, are moving into a universe that suggests entirely new ways of understanding. Just when social scientists seem to have gotten the science down and can construct strings of variables in impressive formulae, the scientists have left, plunging ahead into the vast "porridge of being" that describes a new reality. (p. 141)

The question continues to haunt us—If our leadership models are based upon scientific principles, and the science has changed, then why have not our leadership models changed? The answer would seem to come from our educational experiences. Institutions of higher learning still teach teachers and future administrators the science of behaviorism and classical physics. [In the last sentence, the term "administrators" was carefully chosen by this author. Universities are preparing administrators rather than leaders. As Sergiovanni (1990, p. 17) has suggested, we are more focused on doing things right than doing the right things. In other words, we are teaching administrators how to administer or manage rather than how to lead.] In chapter 1, behaviorism was defined as the objective study of measurable behaviors, rather than a focus on mental processes. Using a behaviorist framework, a boss or administrator would most likely observe the workers (or students) isolate and control variables, and seek replication in order to make predictions. Things that cannot be quantified (creativity, emotions, problem solving, and thinking) would be ignored. For example, teachers are observed annually by the principal. Very often, these observation tools are checklists where the teachers are observed as to the degree or whether or not they meet certain prescribed teaching behaviors. This is a standardized form that treats all teachers alike. Such nebulous concepts as lesson preparation, individualization, and assessment of learning are largely ignored.

One need not look very far in our educational settings to see further examples that Wheatley described earlier. People are often treated with little respect and dignity. Schools are constantly testing students to measure intelligence, intellectual growth, aptitude, and attitude. We have standardized tests, criteria-referenced tests, norm-referenced tests, surveys, inventories. We categorize children into classroom groupings that have more to do with age than with individual development. We categorize children into special education programs. We hire and place teachers into specialized departments and programs. We control teachers by policies and students by rules that treat everyone alike. We purchase curriculum materials that are highly standardized and "teacher proof."

We keep trying to break down the whole into ever smaller pieces so that we can better understand the whole. But the whole cannot be understood when pieces are taken out. Each piece is so intricately and incomprehensibly interwoven that when one variable is touched, all others are affected. It makes one think of the spider web. When any part of the web is touched, the entire web quivers. One can also visualize the old Chinese proverb, "Cut a blade of grass and the whole world trembles." We cannot hope to isolate information by becoming more microscopic in our viewing. We must become macroscopic. President and CEO of the new AT&T, Alex Mandl, and Assistant Director of Executive Education at AT&T Deepak Sethi have claimed that, "Managers once aligned in a chain of command, are navigating instead a web of interdependent people and interwoven parts. Disturb it anywhere and it vibrates all over" (Mandl & Sethi, 1996, p. 261). Rather than isolating variables, we must look at the whole with all variables interconnected. Education change expert Patrick Dolan (1994) wrote,

If your metaphor is organic—that is to say it is closer to a living organism than to a machine—then everything changes. When you look at a school or school district from this perspective, you see a "whole" system with deeply interconnected sub-systems. Any approach that sees the system as one overarching reality means that . . . it is all interconnected much the way a living system is. (p. 4)

We shall explore this concept more in depth later.

CLASSICAL SCIENCE IS NOT APPROPRIATE
FOR THE STUDY OF OPEN SYSTEMS

Newtonian physics seems an inappropriate approach for leadership, because it is dehumanizing, but it is also an inappropriate model for the administration and study of an organization. Our most prized practices of administration are antithetical to the principles of our founding fathers. "We govern our organizations by valuing, above all else, consistency, control, and predictability" (Block, 1996, p. 8). However, Peter Block went on to warn, "There is an unmistakable contradiction between the democratic values of freedom and independence and the colonial and patriarchal strategies used to manage our organizations" (p. 238).

Our current notions of leadership are based upon flawed mental positions. Stephen Covey explained, "Traditional authoritarian supervision is a Win/Lose paradigm. It's also the result of an overdrawn Emotional Bank Account. If you don't have trust or common vision of desired results, you tend to hover over, check up on, and direct" (1990, p. 224). As classical authoritarian supervision relates to education, Thomas Sergiovanni wrote, "Traditional management theory is based on a view of how schools operate that does not fit the real world very well" (1990, p. 44).

Our schools are still organized using the classical organizational thought model. In chapter 1 classical organizational thought was described as a model with the purpose of efficiency. It requires a routinization of performance. This model is characterized by a specialization of tasks and a standardization of those tasks. There is also an impersonal orientation with a uniqueness of function. This organizational structure resembles a rigid pyramid hierarchy. A clear example of classical leadership existing in contemporary school systems is that of policy formulation. School districts are the epitome of organizations run on policies. There are literally hundreds of policies for such functions as community, administration, business, personnel, students, instruction, new construction, internal board policies, bylaws of the board, and job descriptions. These are designed (in practice) to treat all people, or all situations, alike. We often hear the phrase, "Well, my hands are tied; the policy says . . ." as policies seem to take on a life of their own. The policy takes the personal out of working with personnel. Educational systems thinker, Patrick Dolan (1994) stipulated:

If we deliberately set out to create a model deeply antithetical to team work, we could not have done a better job than this Western orthodoxy. (p. 34)

The Un-Team—It is a non-integrated structure in which groups work in silos of specialization, and individuals compete with one another for power, position, and resources.(p. 30)

Examples of classical organizational practices that are inappropriate are everywhere. School budgets are extremely tight and leave little or no room for individual staff development or curriculum exploration. Even with little flexibility, there is a great deal of bureaucratic paperwork around every corner. Furthermore, bus schedules often seem to determine the beginning and end of the school day. In between bus rides, the day is marked with impersonal bells that signal times to move en masse from one class to the next on a routine schedule that resembles a factory. These schools are quite large in order to provide for efficiency; even the individual classes have pupil-teacher ratios that are less than optimal. Teachers often complain that the sizes of their classes require them to teach to the average level of the class, rather than to the individual needs of all students. In other words, students are treated alike, not as individuals. Education expert, Linda Darling-Hammond explained (1999):

One inheritance from the assembly line is the notion that decision making about curriculum, assessments, school design, and student progress is the purview of those who sit above teachers in a large bureaucracy. Teachers' work consists largely of stamping students with lessons as they pass by, conveyer belt style, from grade to grade and class period to class period. (p. 32)

Behaviorism and classical organizational thought continue to be fundamental to current administration practices in today's schools. Unfortunately, as Block forewarns, "Staff functions [personnel services, business services, pupil services, and curriculum and instruction services] are traditionally parenting" (1996, p. 116) and are not appropriate for reform. However, there is a call for change in the leadership paradigm. Secretary-general of the International Federation of Red Cross and Red Crescent Societies George B. Weber exclaimed, "We must realize that the historic command-structure organization is dead. Even the best military organizations recognize that today" (Weber, cited in Hesselbein, 1996, p. 308).

But there is hope. Indeed, there are other ways for us to view our systems and the people we employ. These newly forming models are more natural and support our intuitions. Wheatley (1994a) elaborated on this point, "All this time, we have created trouble for ourselves in organizations by confusing control with order. . . . If organizations are machines, control makes sense. If organizations are process structures, then seeking to impose control through permanent structure is suicide" (p. 22).

In writing the introduction to Joseph Jaworski's book *Synchronicity: The Inner Path of Leadership*, Peter Senge (1996) penned an excellent conclusion to this line of thinking and a very apt call for change:

> Perhaps our institutions and leadership are, by and large, grounded in a way of thinking about the world that is increasingly obsolete and counterproductive. Perhaps that is why they are falling apart. . . . The new leadership must be grounded in fundamentally new understandings of how the world works. The 16th-century Newtonian mechanical view of the universe, which still guides our thinking, has become increasingly dysfunctional in these times of interdependence and change. (p. 9)

To reiterate, the old science is faulty for the purpose of the study of people and of open systems, and for the purpose of serving as a model for leadership. Classical physics and the other classical sciences are not bad or wrong; in fact, they are ingenious. It's their application by social scientists to social systems that is wrong. You don't measure the efficiency of a gasoline engine with a qualitative case study analysis; and, you don't measure the effectiveness of a school system with a quantitative instrument resulting in a raw score or stanine. Nature is far too complex for crude, single-layered measurements. Fortunately, the science that is needed does exist. It has existed for many years, and perhaps in several forms for many generations. The science is the more intuitive science and mathematics of quantum physics.

POINTS TO PONDER

1. Describe Leslie's struggles in this chapter.
2. What types of similar struggles are you addressing?
3. What are some additional struggles that schools have with traditional models?

4. According to chapter 2, why are the classical sciences not an appropriate way to study people?
5. According to chapter 2, why are the classical sciences not an appropriate way to study open systems?
6. With which assertions do you agree in this chapter?
7. With which assertions do you disagree in this chapter? Why?

CHAPTER 3

Quantum Physics

[Indian philosopher Rabindranath] Tagore says, The lamp contains its oil, which it holds securely in its grasp. . . . Thus it is separate from all objects around itself and is miserly. But when lighted it finds meaning at once; its relation with things far and near is established, and it freely sacrifices its fund of oil to feed the flame. . . . Such a lamp is our self.

—N. Champawat (cited in McGreal, 1995, p. 262)

LESLIE'S LAMENT

It was a windy and cloudy late Saturday morning with a threat of rain when Cindy arrived at Leslie's house. "We might as well be indoors on a day like today," Cindy said.

"That's for sure!" Leslie exclaimed. "Are you ready to get down to business, or . . . ?"

"No, I've got this thing fresh on my mind, and I want to get it straightened out. We can talk over lunch. Is that your usual General Tso's chicken and rice? I'm having pork lo mein. It's all set in the kitchen."

Walking into the kitchen, Cindy said, "Leslie, I pulled together our employee evaluation forms and had one of my clients fax over his employee evaluation form. I asked the travel agency executive who leases the building with us for their employee evaluation form, but they didn't have one. She said that they would like to create one, and that she would like to hear what we are doing."

Leslie replied, "I guess I never thought about how the private sector supervises or evaluates their employees, I guess . . ."

"What do you mean by 'supervise' and 'evaluate'?" interrupted Cindy.

"Hmmm. I have to think on that one. I guess often we just intertwine those words. I guess technically we supervise teachers when we observe them, and evaluation is more of a summative thing at the end of the year. I know that teachers say when the principal comes in to observe them, 'The principal is going to evaluate me today.' But, I don't know. I guess I remember in my graduate class they talked about formative and summative evaluations. Summative evaluations are the traditional end-of-the-year evaluations, while anything we do with the teacher in terms of observations and professional development would be considered formative evaluations."

Cindy listened thoughtfully and then responded, "You know, in most businesses, I don't think there really are what you call formative evaluations—at least not in the sense of observations. I don't go into my employees' offices and watch them talk to clients, at least not with the intent of evaluating them. But we do interact often during the course of the work week, and we are continually giving instant feedback to one another. Maybe that's formative evaluation. But you see, we work so closely together on projects. It's just natural to give feedback. I guess that is not typical in schools."

"True. Maybe this is more difficult to compare than what I thought," Leslie interrupted herself. "On the other hand, our school has two sets of teachers that team teach. And certainly other teachers work closely together on a daily and weekly basis. For example, all the social studies teachers plan together and they all work so closely with the special-ed staff. And one of my art teachers very often plans her units around what the regular-ed teachers are doing in their classrooms. These staff do work closely together—certainly more closely than I do with them."

"I always have trouble eating the last bit of rice out of the box with chopsticks; can you give me a fork?" After finishing her rice and pouring another cup of green tea for her sister and herself, Cindy continued. "Forgive me for this suggestion, Leslie, but perhaps the wrong person is doing the evaluating. Well, not all of it. You would undoubtedly be in the best position to do the summative evaluations, but perhaps—now just hear me out—perhaps the teachers would be the best to provide formative supervision. After all, they work with each other the closest and know best how each other is doing. They are the ones who can provide really substantive feedback. Maybe we should look at it like this—what is the purpose of the formative evaluation, or of supervision?"

"You know how to get to the heart of the matter, don't you? I know that most teachers feel it's to fill a bureaucratic function, or for accountability at best. But the intent is to determine if there are any instructional weaknesses and to address those; and, the intent is to help them become better teachers. . . . I think."

Cindy put her hand on her chin and closed her eyes, looking as if she were deep in reflection, or nodding off from lunch and a less-than-absorbing conversation. With her eyes closed, Cindy quietly said, "Let's go back to the private sector for a moment. A couple of minutes ago, I mentioned that we are continually giving each other feedback. You know, asking why something was done this way, why not another way, where do we go from here, how will we know if this is working, when and how will we decide, and so on. Ninety percent of these conversations are just that—conversations. Things are not always written down, at least not something that goes into someone's personnel file. We constantly give each other feedback, and I think we do a better job because of it."

Cindy continued, "Our marketing corporation has an annual evaluation form—a summative form, if you will. As the supervisor, and I only supervise three assistants, I sit down at the end of each year and basically just write a narrative about my thoughts on how each person has done. I look at his or her past annual evaluations and look at how he or she was evaluated—you know, in terms of what each one was doing, areas for improvement, and goals for the upcoming year. Oh, before I do this, they prepare and give to me a self-evaluation, which is a big help for me. They also provide a customer portfolio for me. This shows the work they have completed since the last evaluation period, as well as work in progress."

"Okay, now I get to ask the question back to you!" Leslie quipped. "What is the purpose of this summative evaluation you do?"

"You learned well, grasshopper," Cindy mocked with a smile. "To be honest, I guess it serves a few purposes. First, if a person has not been meeting his or her goals and has been doing unsatisfactorily, this provides documentation toward improvement or possible dismissal. If that is the case, there will have been other documentation building up—a 'paper trail,' if you will. Second, it provides direction for future growth and goals. Third, it allows me to determine merit and whether a bonus, or how large a bonus, is merited."

"Yeah, bonuses! Educators never get bonuses—not even a Thanks-giving turkey!" Leslie cried.

"You didn't go into teaching for the money. You went into it for the intrinsic rewards, right?"

Leslie turned red and glared at her mischievous sister.

"Just kidding, just kidding. You know, I looked at my last client's personnel evaluation system. They are a much larger corporation and they employ 2,000-plus workers in this area. You know who I'm talk-ing about. Anyway, they use a form for their summative evaluation. It basically serves the purpose my narrative does."

Leslie questioned, "Is that a policy? Or, is it part of the collective bargaining agreement? Did the union agree to it?"

"Well, this is not a policy. This is a standard operating procedure, I guess, for their professional staff—they are not unionized for their pro-fessional staff. Their line workers are unionized, but I don't know how they are evaluated. Anyway, I thought you were interested in evaluat-ing and supervising professional staff."

"Well, yeah, but . . . just go on," Leslie hesitated.

Cindy continued, "This end-of-the-year form has a section for goals for the current reporting period. This is filled out one year prior to the summative conference and is signed by both the supervisor and super-visee. This goal section only allows for three goals, and then leaves space for objectives, activities, resources, and a time line to meet these goals."

"That sounds just like what our principals have to do every year. I guess that's who we consider our professional staff—at least in prac-tice, even though that might be unintentional, but it is what we show in practice."

"That's an interesting point, Leslie." Cindy stopped for a moment and sipped her tea. "This form also has an appendix where the em-ployee writes a personal narrative and can attach any supporting docu-mentation. The next section looks like the first, but it is dated for the next year. There is no place for checking whether the person is recom-mended for rehire or release, or what competency level they are judged to have reached."

"Once again, that sounds fairly close to what our principal evalua-tions are like, but nowhere near what we do for our teaching staff," Leslie said.

"Let me also point out that this large corporation also does periodic evaluations throughout the year. Each new professional staff member gets a ninety-day review after they are first hired. It is more narrative in nature. Then he or she has another three-month review, and from then on every six months."

"I wonder how their employees feel about these evaluations?" Leslie asked. "I mean, do they think it is a pain and that it does not provide them with anything of substance?"

Cindy considered this question for a moment. "I know some of the staff members there. It really depends on who their supervisor is. Some people get really good constructive, growth-oriented feedback—feedback that comes through a true dialogue. Others have supervisors who nitpick and find every little fault. Still others have supervisors who write down only positive things and give no constructive feedback."

"That sure sounds like many of my colleagues," Leslie bemoaned. "Some are so negative and think they have to be 'big brother.' Others are afraid to give any 'criticism' or don't know what to say, so they just write all glowing comments—maybe for motivation. Perhaps some are more deliberate; I just don't know."

Cindy jumped in. "You just said something that triggered a thought for me. I bet you can walk into any teacher's classroom, for evaluation purposes, and just know if they are a good teacher. You can feel it intuitively—in your gut. You don't need fancy forms or checklists."

"Yeah, I think you're right." Leslie got up to clear off the table and wash the dishes. "It seems to me that I have to treat my faculty more like professionals. More interaction and feedback among them. Maybe my role will be changing. Maybe I need to provide opportunities for them to get together, to reflect, and to provide for their own professional growth as colleagues."

"Go, girl!"

"Maybe I will have to create their schedules so they will have routine time to get together and plan and reflect. But I guess the first step is for us to start talking. We need to get together as professional colleagues and decide how we can together make this system more growth-oriented. That's the first step, wouldn't you think?"

"That's the plan, Cindy!" Leslie exclaimed. "I feel good, so good. Just like I knew that I would!" Leslie sang as she did her best James Brown impersonation. "Oh, I digress. Anyway, this has got me thinking about so many other things. Next month we can get together and talk about staff development. How about Tex-Mex?"

THE SCIENCE

The primary focus of classical physics and the primary focus of quantum physics and their respective impact on leadership practices are contrary to one another. "The Newtonian model of the world is characterized by materialism and reductionism—a focus on things rather than relationships. . . . In the new science, the underlying currents are . . . giving primary value to the relationships that exist among seemingly discrete parts" (Wheatley, 1994a, p. 9). Professors of medicine at the University of Arizona Gary Schwartz and Linda Russek (1999) provide an easy intimation of the differences between Newtonian physics (reductionist science) and quantum mechanics (general systems science):

- Whereas reductionist science assumes that things are *independent*, general systems science assumes that things are *interdependent* and hence *integrative*.
- Whereas reductionist science assumes that things are *disconnected*, general systems science assumes that things are *interconnected* to various degrees.
- Whereas reductionist science assumes that things can be understood in *isolation*, general systems science assumes that things can only be understood when they are *allowed to interact freely*. [all emphases are in original] (p. 35)

The author of *Art and Physics* and *The Alphabet Versus the Goddess,* Leonard Shlain, wrote a wonderful description of how the classical sciences transitioned into eventually the new era of quantum physics and how these sciences began to change society. He spoke of electromagnetism and how it forced us to change our views of nature (1998):

Electromagnetism is not confined to one bounded locus in space. It is not mechanistic as it has no moving parts. It is not reducible and can only be apprehended in its totality. It is a pattern rather than a point, insubstantial rather than material, more a verb than a noun, more a process than an object, more sinuous than angular. . . . The words used to describe it, such as "web," "matrix," "waves," and "strands," are all words etymologically and mythologically associated with the feminine. A "field," which has proved to be electromagnetism's most common synonym, is a noun borrowed from agriculture and nature. Electromagnetism had an organic interdependence, and it supplanted the Mechanical Age's independent steps, sequence, and specialization with holism, simultaneity, and integration. The great principle at the heart of electromagnetism is that tension exists between polar opposites: positive and negative. An electromagnetic state only exists when both are present. The two poles, positive and negative, always strive to unite and it is only when they do that energy is generated. (p. 385)

Yes, this was the mark of a new age in scientific thinking. However, it was only the transition. Quantum physics and the other new sciences ushered in the new age. Perhaps they only ushered in the new age of scientific thinking. Practitioners in the social science fields have been slow to learn. Let's now turn our attention from this transition to the newer sciences.

Just what is quantum physics? Quantum physics can best be defined as a "statistical theory that deals with probabilities" (Stapp, 1993, p. 14). It looks at the interconnectedness of the universe at the subatomic level. Its language is the more intuitive and qualitative mathematics of patterns and relationships. Theoretical physicist and Director of the Center for Ecoliteracy in Berkeley, California, Fritjof Capra (1996) stipulated:

In the formalism of quantum theory these relationships are expressed in terms of probabilities, and the probabilities are determined by the dynamics of the whole system. Whereas in classical mechanics the properties and behavior of the parts determine those of the whole, the situation is reversed in quantum mechanics: it is the whole that determines the behavior of the parts. (p. 31)

In other words, the parts are so intertwined with all the other parts that their very existence, nature, and behavior are in large part governed by the whole system. When viewing a part in isolation, the observer does not see the part as it really exists. The part behaves differently when it is isolated than it does when it is integrated with the whole. This may remind the reader of the ancient Sufi story of six blind men who happen upon an elephant. Each blind man reaches out to touch a different part of the elephant. One man feels the oak-like stature of the elephant's leg, while another feels the heavy coarse skin. Still another man holds the elephant's strong and flexible trunk, while another holds its small and ropelike tail. Similarly, another man feels the rigid tusks, and another feels its expansive and thin ears. Each man has certainly felt the elephant, but knows not an elephant. In isolation, each part is different, but does not show the true essence of what it is to be an elephant. When all the parts are living and breathing together, we can have a better view of what it is to be an elephant. As Anaxagoras said, "All things will be in everything; nor is it possible for them to be apart, but all things have a portion of everything."

The findings of quantum physics and other new sciences tell us that:

(1) with a duality in nature, there is also complementarity and uncertainty,
(2) people and systems are subjective and cannot be observed objectively,
(3) all of nature is unified and interconnected,
(4) a web of relationships is central to this unification,
(5) changes at the local level can make huge impacts at the system level, and
(6) what might appear to be chaos, may not actually be chaos but may be an underlying order.

Let us now briefly examine several experiments and how their findings impact leadership. There are a few theoretical experiments that will be central to the understanding of these principles of quantum mechanics. (Several experiments from other new sciences will be provided in chapter 4).

DOUBLE SLIT EXPERIMENT

According to theoretical physicist and cofounder of string field theory Michio Kaku (1997, p. 107), "One of the essential postulates of the quantum theory is that matter can exhibit both wavelike and particle-like characteristics," all at the same time. The double slit experiment proves this postulate. The following description will briefly explain this actual experiment. Imagine a light beam pointed directly at a vertical surface. The surface has two slits that can allow the light beam to pass through it, either through one slit at a time or through both slits simultaneously. There is a recording device behind the surface; this device measures whether the light behaves like individual particles or is diffuse representing wavelike characteristics. If only one slit is open, the light will land on the recording device and be measured as individual particles. If both slits are open, the light will land on the recording device and be measured as a wave. What makes the experiment so confounding is the fact that the light beam behaves in such a way as to suggest it knows whether one or both slits are open, and even more confounding, that it is being observed. The light coming in is both a wave and particles, at the same time. This concept, theorized by Niels Bohr, is known as the Principle of Complementarity, wherein light contains dualistic attributes—particles and waves. But, because of the experiment and the observation, it collapses into one or the other state. If not observed, it would continue being both wavelike and particlelike.

If this still seems unclear, perhaps a more detailed description and a diagram would be of assistance (see figure 3.1). It is important to remember that particles are real objects. They do have an actual physical location. But waves are not objects. Waves are "an event or phenomenon" (Pine, 2000, p. 216). One might want to think of waves on a body of water—they are much more of a phenomenon than a separate thing. With only minor modifications, the following descriptions and diagrams come from the work of Ronald Pine (2000, pp. 218–224):

> Imagine first a lead box impenetrable except for two microscopic slits on one side. On the inside of the box on the side opposite the slits is a photographic film. Imagine that on the outside facing the two slits we have a source of radiation, beams of electrons or light, and that we aim this radiation at the face of the box with the two slits. By looking at the kind of exposure that results on the photographic film, we can deduce what kind of radiation is penetrating the box. For instance, if the radiation consists of beams of particles, then only those particles that happen to be aligned with the two slits will pass through into the box, and the result should be a "particle effect." The photographic film should show a diffused piling up of little hits adjacent to the two slits.
>
> On the other hand, if radiation is a wave, then a much different effect should result. We should see a "wave effect," roughly what we would see if we dropped two stones in the water at the same time. Two circular undulations would collide into each other and interfere with each other. In our example, a wave would split in two as it enters the two slits, and then the two new waves would begin to spread out again, eventually colliding with each other as in our pond example. This should cause an "interference effect," a wave picture, on the photographic film. Instead of a piling effect adjacent to the two slits, the radiation would spread throughout the length of the photographic film, producing alternating bands of exposure. Some of the wave crests would meet and accentuate each other. The exposed bands on the photographic film would be the result of the crests meeting.
>
> If light is a wave (a), then a series of alternating light and dark fringes should appear on a photographic film after the light is made to pass

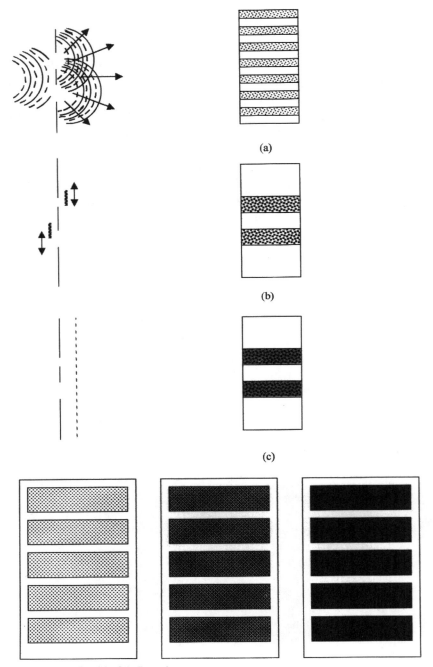

Figure 3.1   Double Slit Experiment

through a pair of slits. This can be explained by "picturing" a set of circular waves starting from each slit. Where the waves intersect, they are reinforced, producing maximum light intensity and the banding effect on the film. The banding effect appears regardless of the intensity of the light.

If light consists of tiny particles (b), then a single pair of bright stripes should appear on the film. If alternate slits are opened and closed, this picture is actually recorded.

If a detection device is added to the arrangement in (a) with both slits open, then the picture in (c) is actually recorded. That is, we see a particle effect.

In fact, closer inspection of the film in (a) that appears to show a wave effect also shows a gradual piling up of individual particle hits (d).

From *Science and the human prospect* (pp. 218–224) by Ronald C. Pine. Belmont, CA: Wadsworth Publishing. Copyright 2000 by Ronald C. Pine. Reprinted with permission.

Our Newtonian way of thinking has led us to believe that atoms can only be particles or only wavelike at any given moment, not both simultaneously. In reality, they are both particles and wavelike concurrently. Niels Bohr found no problem with this duality in nature. He coined the phrase "complementarity" to explain the notion that nature needs both sides of this coin. They are different but not separate. Both need one another—they complement each other. However, our observations limit our views and perceptions to seeing only one of the concurrent aspects at a time. Shlain (1998) explained that the natural world is filled with this duality and complementarity. We can talk of right-brained and left-brained thinking. While one hemisphere may dominate, both work together to complement one another. He went further when he posited that this dualistic thinking has impacted our world cultures. The Western world is known for its linear and rational thinking, while the Eastern world is known more for its holistic thinking. Shlain wrote:

An important factor affecting a culture's historical development is the ability to grasp the concept of the individual. The reductionist aspect inherited in alphabets, called spelling, has encouraged users of this form to see themselves apart from nature, their deity, their governments, and each other. In contrast, the pattern recognition inherent in ideographic language has enmeshed users in a web of interpersonal relationships. The patterns in their language have kept them bound to their institutions, not separate from them. (p. 185)

The Heisenberg Uncertainty Principle shows us a conundrum of our classical approach to studying nature. Since we know that any thing has multiple characteristics, and since we know that we can only study one aspect at a time, we will never be able to understand or observe the entire system as a "unified whole" (Wheatley, 1994a, p. 35). "Heisenberg's remarkable discovery was," according to Gary Zukav—author of *The Dancing Wu Li Masters*—(1980, p. 111), "that there are limits beyond which we cannot measure accurately. . . . There exists an ambiguity barrier beyond which we never can pass without venturing into the realm of uncertainty . . . the 'uncertainty principle.'"

Similarly, there is the concept known as quantum mechanical tunneling. In classical physics, items such as atoms move from one place to another place in a linear fashion. However, quantum physics has shown how an atom "can go from the inside of a bottle to the outside without removing the top, or breaking the bottle; without punching a hole in it, or squeezing past the fork," according to physicist Evan Harris Walker (2000, p. 217). Quantum mechanical tunneling exists because things in the subatomic world live in bundles of potentialities. They move in ways different than our usual senses.

If this all seems too incomprehensible, the reader can take solace in these words of quantum physicist Niels Bohr, "Anyone who is not shocked by the quantum theory does not understand it" (cited in Kaku, 1997, p. 265). But the message is clear—there is more than one way to view and understand nature, and objectivity is an illusion. Ronald Pine (2000) wrote:

> According to Bohr, nature reveals this to us by showing that we can have only complementary views of reality. If we set up an experimental arrangement to view subatomic phenomena as particles, then that is what we will observe. . . . In short, an electron is not a thing until we observe it! (p. 226)

Still, the reader might ask, "Might we humans also, in some mysterious way, have both particle-like individuality and wave-like shared beings and interconnectedness?" (Gilman, 1993, p. 12).

SCHRODINGER'S CAT

Schrodinger's Cat has created a dilemma for quantum physicists as well. Austrian physicist Erwin Schrodinger designed an imaginary or theoretical experiment wherein a live cat was placed inside a metal box. The box is enclosed in such a way that no one can see what is happening inside the box. A mechanism triggers the release of either food or deadly cyanide gas–producing pellets. Now the conundrum. Through mathematical figuring—known as a "probability function"—that is beyond the scope of this book, Schrodinger showed that after the trigger has released its food or poison the cat is both alive and dead at the same time, that is until the observer opens the box. At the instant of observation, the cat is then observed as either alive or dead and the alternate chance is gone forever.

Schrodinger's Cat has now become a reality. While there is no real cat, the theoretical construct has now been proven in physics laboratories. Gary Taubes (1996) reported that physicists at the National Institute of Standards and Technology in Boulder, Colorado, have been able to:

> trap a single beryllium ion in an electromagnetic cage, excite it into a superposition of internal electronic quantum states, then ease those two states apart so that the atom appears to be in two distinct physical locations simultaneously. The result can be considered the anti-vivisectionist version of the dead-and-alive superposition of cat states. (p. 1101)

As has been described earlier as packets of potentialities, atoms can occupy several different orbits at one time. This complementarity principle has been coupled together with Schrodinger's Cat. Philip Yam (1997) reported similar work by David Pritchard and other physicists at the Massachusetts Institute of Technology. With the use of lasers, these scientists have been able to cool atoms and move them around. In Yam's words:

> Physicists have . . . created small-scale Schrodinger's cats. These "cats" were individual electrons and atoms made to reside in two places simultaneously, and electromagnetic fields excited to vibrate in two different ways at once. (p. 124)

These findings reinforce the idea of potentialities. Everything exists simultaneously as a packet of potentialities. Quantum physicists call this "the state vector." This is the point in which something is suspended in all its potential phases. However, at the point of observation, we get "state vector collapse," or the point in which all the possible outcomes collapse into one state—the state that we see. Again, there is more than one way to view and understand nature, and each thing or action does not exist as only one reality until the act of observation. In other words, the observer and the act of observation help to create reality. By our very act of observation, we help to create reality. We lose more when we make an observation or measurement; we miss more than we see. What's more, we might not even be able to make critical judgments about the differences of what we measure. One final idea is this area of duality is the notion of inseparability. Inseparability is the notion that two "identical particles . . . have no separate identity. There is no way in which one can place a sign on one of these particles in order to distinguish it from another of the same type" (Walker, 2000, p. 71). So, not only can our observations be muddled because what we are observing may be two things at once, but now we can't even for certain say two apparently separate objects are indeed separate. What does all this say for our testing and assessments?

BELL'S THEOREM

In another experiment, nonlocal causality—or Bell's Theorem—we learn that relationships and interconnectedness are the foundation of all systems. In this theoretical experiment, designed by physicist John Bell and later demonstrated in the laboratory by Thomas Young, two electrons are paired together and given the identical spin on their axes. When they are separated over a great distance in space and then measured, they still have the same spin. However, if after they are separated, one is given a new spin, the other one will simultaneously change its spin accordingly, on its own. This would suggest that they are communicating over space and time, a time that is faster than the speed of light. Zukav (1980, p. 293) wrote, "In 1972 John Clauser and Stuart Freedman of the Lawrence Berkeley Laboratory actually performed this experiment to confirm or disprove these predictions. They found that the statistical predictions upon which Bell based his theorem *are* correct."

What follows is an analogy that might make Bell's Theorem more easily understood—as described by Ronald C. Pine (2000, pp. 231–232):

Suppose we have a large group of runners. Half of the runners are tall and half are short. Suppose that each of the short runners and each of the tall runners has a twin. Each of the twins will begin running at the same point, but in the opposite direction to a finish line that is the same distance from the original point of departure. Suppose also that each runner will run the course at the same speed, and that the spacing between the times when each runner leaves is such that no runner will be able to overtake the runner immediately preceding him. No tall runners will overtake short runners or vice versa.

Imagine then a continuous stream of runners leaving the original point and running in opposite directions. We might have something like this: Two short runners leave the starting point one after the other simultaneous with their respective twins, then two tall, then two short again, then one tall, and one short after that, then two tall, and so on. Suppose that the overall pattern is random. Suppose further that the contingencies of the course and the physical training of each runner are such that many of the runners will not finish. Suppose also that each twin has a very strong desire to finish, such that any one twin will want to finish if and only if the other twin finishes.

Now we are ready to carry out the implications of our thought experiment. In spite of the strong desire of each twin to finish if and only if the other does, our common sense would predict that finishing together is not likely. Suppose one of the short runners pulls a muscle just before the finish line. How likely would it be that the twin, running on an independent track, separated by a considerable distance, either knows this and decides to stop running or pulls a muscle and also does not finish? In other words, if we were to observe the runners finishing and established a mathematical correlation of completion, we would not expect it to be very high. Suppose that about 90 percent of the tall and short runners did not finish; it would not be very likely that every time a short or taller runner finished or did not finish, the respective twin finished or did not finish as well. If we found the random result at one finish likely to be T, T, S, T, S, S, T, S, we would not expect this result to be highly correlated or equal to the result at the other finish line. We would expect an inequality in the results. But, in this imaginary race, the results *are* correlated. The twins do finish in corresponding order. They are communicating over time and space.

So, the paradox exists. It would seem to be impossible for the runners (or the atoms) to communicate instantaneously at such a great distance. But as Pine himself concludes, "We *assume* [emphasis added] that the runners are independent individuals who will face independent conditions at independent places" (2000, p. 232). Pine (2000, p. 233) then ties this loose end up by stating, "If the movement of one object 'instantaneously' influences the movement of another object, then they are not really separate objects." In *Synchronicity: The Inner Path of Leadership,* Joseph Jaworski (1996, p. 79) writes, "The effect is a simple consequence of the oneness of apparently separate objects. It is a quantum loophole through which physics admits the necessity of a unitary vision." Furthermore, "*relationship* is the key determiner of what is observed and of how particles manifest themselves. Particles come into being and are observed only in relationship to something else. They do not exist as independent 'things'" (Wheatley, 1994a, p. 10).

Thinking in this quantum world is very confusing to our three-dimensional view. Physicists often tell a story of a funny world. Imagine a two-dimensional world called Flatland. All objects in this world are flat. Houses are flat, tables and chairs, and people are flat. So, all objects look like squares, triangles, circles, and so on. Nobody has ever seen anything, or even imagined anything, that is three-dimensional. Words such as up, down, above, over, under have no meaning to flatlanders. People think in terms of next to, beside, and around.

Now think for a moment if you, from the three-dimensional world, entered a flatlander's world. Would a flatlander be able to see you in three dimensions? The answer is no. Flatlanders would only be able to see a slice of you, a two dimension of you. They would understand a different truth or reality of you. (But of course, we know the real truth or reality.) If for some reason you were able to communicate with them, it would be quite difficult for you to explain your world, your three-dimensional world. They would have great difficulty understanding and believing our three-dimensional world. Perhaps this is similar to trying to explain how a sunset looks to a person who has never seen, or how Handel's Messiah sounds to someone who has never heard before. The two-dimensional world is real and so is the three-dimensional world. Thinking in the quantum world is outside our regular vocabulary and our learned *common sense*. But, if we can be comfortable with this confusion and uncertainty, we can learn some valuable lessons. "The point to think about is that when we make a measurement . . . when the observed system interacts with the observing system—we reduce a multi-dimensional reality to a three-dimensional reality compatible with our experience" (Zukav, 1980, p. 76). Zukav even postulated that if we could see the fourth dimension of time we would be able to see the past, the present, and the future all at once.

Again, as in both the double slit experiment and Schrodinger's Cat, we learn that the observer and the observed are totally interconnected—one does not exist without the other, and that existence is changed because of this relationship. "John Wheeler, a well-known physicist at Princeton, wrote: . . . . 'Participator' is the incontrovertible new concept given by quantum mechanics. It strikes down the term 'observer' of classical theory, the man who stands safely behind the thick glass wall and watches what goes on without taking part," (Zukav, 1980, p. 28). Pine (2000) bemoaned:

> Western civilization and its science . . . has assumed that the cosmos consists of one distinct complete reality full of details. We have also assumed that the details, whatever they might be, can be known, and knowing these details does not affect what the details actually are independent of the knower. (p. 225)

Even more so, "Bell's theorem implies, at a quantum level, that the physical world is an inseparable whole" (Gilman, 1993, p. 12). Furthermore, people are not separate from the world. We cannot sit outside the natural system and not have an impact. A principal observing a teacher clearly impacts the lesson. The principal/observer is really a "participator." Finally, we learn of the primacy of relationships and of the interconnectedness of nature. As Robert Gilman (1993, p. 11) posited, "We—like all of the physical universe—are inescapably linked at a quantum mechanical level."

WHY THE QUANTUM PHYSICS APPROACH IS BETTER FOR UNDERSTANDING PEOPLE

Again, classical physics is an inappropriate approach for the framing of educational leadership models. "Traditional management theory is based on a view of how schools operate that does not fit the real world very well" (Sergiovanni, 1990, p. 44). After a meeting with Japanese businessmen, Joseph Jaworski (1996) reflected:

> I was struck, however, from the very outset at how rational the Westerners in the group seemed to be, and how skeptical and even disdainful most of them were of anything that smacked of what they referred to as 'the soft stuff'—anything that could not be measured or quantified. Graphs and charts were the order of the day because quantification and measurement were what was seen as real. . . . I had come to see the immeasurable as precisely that which was most real, that which I cared

most deeply about. I recalled what [quantum physicist] Bohm had said about this, "The attempt to suppose that measure exists prior to man and independently of him leads, as has been seen, to the 'objectivication' of man's insight so that it becomes rigidified and unable to change, eventually bringing about fragmentation and general confusion." (p. 151)

It seems that the scientific method and the objectification of things has made our institutions so very sterile. Workers have known this for decades, and social scientists and theorists have been calling for changes. Russian psychiatrist Mihaly Csikszentmihalyi (1990, p. 78) warned, "The evidence suggests that the Industrial Revolution not only shortened the life spans of members of several generations, but made them more nasty and brutish as well." Diane Fassel (leadership expert) wrote about the confusion of our organizations, "Perhaps some of the disequilibrium we are feeling in organizations is that the old organizational diagram is hardwired in our brains, while the actual process we experience is one of relationships" (Fassel, 1998, p. 218). In a somewhat different vein, Margaret Wheatley (1994a, p. 12) wrote, "We are refocusing on the deep longings we have for community, meaning, dignity, and love in our organizational lives . . . rather than . . . believing that we can confine workers into narrow roles, as though they were cogs in machinery of production."

Intuition is central to quantum mechanics. Educators, though, have been late to realize that intuition is important to leadership. Some of the most highly successful private-sector leaders have known this. Leadership theorist Peter Senge (1990) posited:

Intuition in management has recently received increasing attention and acceptance, after many decades of being officially ignored. Now numerous studies show that experienced managers and leaders rely heavily on intuition—that they do not figure out complex problems rationally. They rely on hunches, recognize patterns, and draw intuitive analogies and parallels to other seemingly disparate situations. . . . Their intuitions tell them that cause and effect are not close in time and space, that obvious solutions will produce more harm than good, and that short-term fixes produce long-term problems. (p. 168)

From Confucius to Radhakrishnan to Toju and others, many ancient Eastern philosophers had cherished intuition, as well. In fact, Sarvepalli Radhakrishnan believed that "intuition enables us to know Reality directly" (Champawat, 1995, p. 279). Likewise, the feeling of the interconnectedness of the universe "is central to every major religion, including Judaism, Islam, Christianity, Hinduism, Buddhism, and Taoism" (Jaworski, 1996, p. 57). According to Pine (2000, p. 245), "Eastern mysticism is also consistent with the results of quantum physics. The mystics have always rejected the idea of a hidden clockwork mechanism, sitting out there, independent of human observation." This interconnectedness is crucial to the survival of our organizations and systems. "At the heart of a learning organization is a shift of mind—from seeing ourselves separate from the world to connected to the world" (Senge, 1990, p. 12). At the subatomic level Capra (1996, p. 30) explained, "In quantum theory we never end up with any 'things;' we always deal with interconnections." In terms of how this relates to organizations, Capra put forth, "In nature there is no 'above' or 'below,' and there are no hierarchies. There are only networks nesting within other networks" (p. 35).

The interconnectedness in nature and in organizations then tells of the importance of relationships. From quantum physics we learn that "Molecules and atoms—the structures described by quantum physics—consist of components. However, these components, the subatomic particles, cannot be understood as isolated entities but must be defined through interrelations" (Capra, 1996, p. 30). Margaret Wheatley connected quantum physics to management by stating, "Leadership is now being examined for its relational aspects. . . . If the physics of our universe is revealing the primacy of relationships, is it any wonder that we are beginning to reconfigure our ideas about management in relational terms?" (1994a, p. 12). Systems thinkers from Covey to Csikszentmihalyi and from Senge to Block have seen the vital importance of relationships. Joseph Jaworski (1996, p. 57) said, "The organizing principle of the universe is 'relatedness.'" Indeed, interconnectedness and relationships are the hallmark of systems thinking. In the words of Patrick Dolan (1994):

> The first issue of systems-thinking is that the critical phenomena are *not* [emphasis in original] the individual parts, but how they fit together. This is a network of relationships deeply interconnected. Each one of these "sub-systems" is somehow defined by the position of the others. (p. 63)

It would appear quantum physics does seem to be a better match for creating a model of leadership, for working with humans rather than automatons. Quantum physics speaks of relations, interconnectedness, and the intuition of humans. Before we turn our attention to lessons that can be learned for educational leadership, it is appropriate to spend some time learning about the other new sciences.

POINTS TO PONDER

1. How is Leslie addressing her problem of teacher supervision/evaluation?
2. What is the primary issue with which you are dealing at work (in terms of classical organizations)?
3. How are you (or will you) planning to address it?
4. Describe the double slit experiment. What do we learn from it?
5. Describe Schrodinger's Cat. What do we learn from it?
6. Describe Bell's Theorem. What do we learn fom it?
7. Why would the new sciences be more appropriate for us to use to understand people and open systems?
8. How could Leslie, or you, use something learned from quantum mechanics to address her problem, or your issue, described in question 2 above?

CHAPTER 4

The Other New Sciences

This we know. All things are connected like the blood which unites one family. . . . Whatever befalls the earth, befalls the sons and daughters of the earth. Man did not weave the web of life; he is merely a strand in it. Whatever he does to the web, he does to himself.

—Ted Perry (inspired by Chief Seattle, cited in Capra, 1996, p. xi)

LESLIE'S LAMENT

Leslie returned to school on Monday. She had decided to complete Mary Thompson's observation report in the manner that she usually did; she would hold her postconference after school that day. Still, something was bothering her, and she couldn't put her finger on it. Leslie had the feeling that observing and evaluating teachers in isolation was a disservice to the teachers as it missed out on the complexity of the teaching environment. After all, teachers didn't work totally in isolation. They worked within the context of the building's culture and in that of the community; they worked within the norms of the other teachers, and they had to work within the parameters of the individual and collective needs of the students. How could you isolate teaching to one classroom at a time? Weren't teachers embedded within the system? Indeed, when we were evaluating a teacher, weren't we evaluating the whole system? She felt uncomfortable with the fact that it seemed inappropriate to observe and evaluate a teacher in isolation. There were so many variables. The teacher was a part of a larger system. Leslie wrote a memo to the staff briefly reporting on her frustration with the current method of teacher observation and evaluation. She further wrote about her conversation with Cindy, and that she would like to have a faculty meeting on Wednesday after school to discuss this issue, and only this issue. She asked the teachers to bring ideas. "We're getting off the dime," Leslie thought to herself.

In order to maintain the meaningful spirit of her Saturday dialogue with Cindy, Leslie bought two dozen egg rolls and tea for the teachers. She was excited, yet a little nervous. After the faculty assembled, Leslie quickly reviewed the contents of the memo. She opened up the meeting for input.

Silence.

More silence.

This was supposed to be inspirational, Leslie thought in frustration. "Does anybody like our present system of observations and evaluations?" she asked.

The silence was broken only by the clacking of teacups. Finally, uncomfortable with the silence, Tom Brentley spoke up. "I don't want to evaluate my friends. That is your job." Several heads nodded in agreement, and several other heads munched on egg rolls.

"Okay. This is good. . . ." Leslie stuttered in disbelief.

After another pause, Leslie continued. "Are your summative evaluations meaningful to you?"

"What is a summative evaluation?" asked Samantha, a rookie teacher.

"Oh, that's the annual end-of-the-year evaluation I write for each teacher. Have they been meaningful to anybody?" Several heads looked timidly down at their tables.

Tom got up and poured himself some more tea, and motioned as if to ask if anyone else wanted any.

"Let me try another direction," Leslie stammered. "Does anyone find my observations worthwhile?" More reaction this time. Several younger teachers politely nodded, while numerous other teachers smiled in amusement.

Finally, Mary Thompson spoke up. "I think the input you can give to newer teachers is necessary and appropriate. They need to know if they are doing a good job and to be given direction for improvement. But if I may speak for some of my veteran colleagues, the observations become less and less meaningful to us. They are more . . . more . . ."

"An interruption in our busy days!" Gavin Jenkins interjected.

This was catching Leslie off-guard, but then she remembered that she too was frustrated and wanted to make a change. "You are all sharing the same frustrations I have. I do believe that I can provide some feedback to everyone, but I don't think it is adequate or sufficient."

"I can see your point," piped up Sarah Lesofsky, a music teacher. "But how can we make some changes? Like Tom said, I don't want to evaluate my peers."

Leslie thought for a moment. "You know, I think we have to define for ourselves the terms 'supervision' and 'evaluation.' Evaluation, to me, means that someone has determined whether or not you are doing acceptable work in order to keep working here. In other words, whether you are meeting performance standards, or not. Does that make sense to you?"

Although there was silence, most heads nodded in agreement. The silence was broken by the staff clown, Frank Teal, who asked, "Are you going to feed us at each faculty meeting?"

Without missing a beat, Peg O'Brien said, "You can feed yourself, Teal!"

"All right, all right, but seriously," Frank replied, "what about our current evaluation that has five categories in nine areas to be checked? You know, 'exceeds expectations,' 'above expectations,' 'meets expectations,' 'needs improvement,' and 'you're fired.'"

"Well, what do you think? Do you like that?" Leslie asked.

"No, and it doesn't fit your definition of evaluation," Frank retorted.

"That's my definition. For this to be effective, we need a collective definition," Leslie replied.

"Can I interrupt?" asked Betty Bower, an LD teacher. "I know I speak for all my friends here, and I know you truly care, so I say this with all due respect. You are the fourth principal we have had in the last nine years. How can a principal evaluate me or anyone when they only observe us three times a year in the years when we are being supervised? And, what's more, how can you determine any growth? By the time my three-year cycle comes up again, you will probably be a central-office administrator. The only people who really know me and can see my growth are my peers."

"You said that better that I could, Betty," Leslie replied. "Perhaps I need to give my definition of supervision. I would define supervision as a method for professionals to work together in order to provide for professional growth. Here's where one professional talks about curriculum or pedagogy or assessment with another professional or professionals.

They meet to discuss what they are doing and how they can help one another. The observation can be the vehicle for one or more professionals to watch their colleagues work on this professional growth. I know that sounds too much like a textbook. But, I guess what I mean is that supervision means one professional helping another to become a better teacher. It doesn't necessarily have to be with the observation form we are currently using. There are many techniques that one person can use to observe another, and I can share these with you. And we don't only have to think of supervision as observation. Supervision can include other areas in professional development."

Sensing she was rambling, Leslie concluded with, "Tell you what. I will go make some more tea. If you all could spend the next forty minutes in small groups discussing these issues. . . . Wait, let's not bite off more than we can chew. Let's save the summative evaluations for another time. Let's focus on how we can make observations or teacher supervision more meaningful."

Over the next forty minutes things progressed satisfactorily. The teachers were on the task at hand, but perhaps less enthusiastically than Leslie had hoped. Still, she knew progress was slow and painstaking at times. At the end of the forty minutes, the small groups reported back to the main group. Much of the discussion was similar between the groups, but a few interesting points came forth.

Mary Thompson spoke for her group. "We would like to see what you have for different techniques to observe teachers. We mean that we want to see how else we can be observed rather than using our traditional observation form."

Ben Garza voiced a concern common to all groups, "We would like to maybe observe and work more with each other, but where is the time? I simply don't have the time to preconference, observe, and postconference with all my colleagues. Where do we get the time for all this? Maybe that's why principals do it. What it lacks in effectiveness, it makes up for inefficiency." Laughter rolled across the tables.

Leslie quickly interjected, "If it is ineffective, how can it be efficient? We get nowhere fast, and ruin morale in the meantime."

"As building rep for our collective bargaining unit," Hannah Sargent said, "this is a good discussion, but I don't know if our contract will permit this."

Tom Brentley interrupted, "I don't see why not. We won't be evaluating each other! Right, Les?"

Leslie just smiled. She wasn't sure how to respond.

A reading teacher, Vicki Gibson, raised her hand. "You know, the end of the day is upon us. And I hate to think of another committee, but I would be willing to look into this if others were interested."

Mike Tippler, a phys. ed. teacher, said, "Me, too." Leslie made eye contact with a couple of teachers. Mike always wants to work on committees with Vicki.

"I'll work with them," Mary Thompson added.

"And I'll chaperone," muttered Hannah, amid the giggles of a few of her colleagues and blushes of Vicki. Mike didn't even notice as he cracked his knuckles.

Leslie wrapped up the meeting. "Okay, I'll work with you and we'll report back at the next faculty meeting in October." She walked off humming to herself the theme song from *Caddyshack*, "I'm all right, don't nobody worry about me. . . ."

THE SCIENCE

While quantum physics has given us a whole new lens through which to look at life and systems, what we are learning from other sciences is no less intriguing. From chaos theory to chemistry and from fractals to the science of complexity and the study of ecosystems, we are learning many new lessons that should dramatically change the way we work with people and the way in which we organize our educational systems.

CHAOS THEORY AND THE SCIENCE OF COMPLEXITY

When most of us went to school we learned that in classical thermodynamics a system's optimal level is equilibrium. In other words, all systems strive for equilibrium or homeostasis. There is no change. This is precisely for what we are always striving in our organizations. We wish to maintain consistency and control where everything is at a state of equilibrium. However, in chaos theory (also known as dynamical systems theory) we learn that equilibrium is a state of entropy—the state where systems begin to die. When a system is at equilibrium, it cannot change, it begins to entropy, and it dies. But when a system fluctuates and makes changes, it *appears* to be in disorder or in chaos. Yet, as Capra (1996, p. 190) posited, "In the new science of complexity, which takes its inspiration from the web of life, we learn that nonequilibrium is a source of order." The apex where the situation or experiment may either fall into true and total disarray, or evolve into a higher level of order is called the bifurcation point. This is the point at which the system will either die or reorganize into a higher level. This happens in the lab, in nature, and in open systems.

The following is an excellent laboratory example borrowed directly from Gary Zukav in *The Dancing Wu Li Masters* (1980, pp. 306–307):

Imagine a large hollow cylinder into which is placed a smaller cylinder. The space between the smaller cylinder and the larger cylinder is filled with a clear viscous liquid like glycerine (such a device actually exists).

Now suppose that we deposit a small droplet of ink on the surface of the glycerine. Because of the nature of the glycerine, the ink drop remains intact, a well-defined black spot floating on a clear liquid. (See figure 4.1.)

If we begin to rotate one of the cylinders, say in a clockwise direction, the drop of ink spreads out in the opposite direction, making a line which grows thinner and thinner until it disappears altogether. The ink droplet

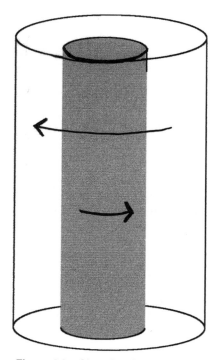

Figure 4.1   Glycerine Cylinder

now is enfolded completely into the glycerine, *but it is still there.* When we rotate the cylinder in the opposite direction, the ink droplet reappears. A fine line appears which grows thicker and thicker and then collects into a single point.

If we continue the counterclockwise motion of the cylinder, the same thing happens, but in reverse. We can repeat this process as often as we like. Each time the ink spot becomes a fine line and disappears into the glycerine only to reappear again when the motion of the glycerine is reversed.

If it requires one complete revolution of the cylinder clockwise to make the droplet disappear completely, once complete revolution of the cylinder counterclockwise will make it reappear in its original shape and location. The number of revolutions required to make the droplet disappear or reappear is the enfolded order. Bohm calls this enfolded order the "implicate order," which means the same thing.

While an example of bifurcation is easy to illustrate in the laboratory, other examples of bifurcation exist in our social systems. The fall of communism in the former Soviet Union is just such an example. The civil rights movement and the social upheaval of the Vietnam War are still other examples in our own nation's history. Education is currently seeing unmistakable signs of bifurcation and chaos as we move farther and farther from equilibrium. The signs are the external movements toward charter schools, schools of choice, the standards movement, teacher licensure advocacy, high-stakes testing, and the quintessential back-to-basics movement.

As has been mentioned earlier in this book, human organizations are not closed systems like machines. Rather they are open systems. Natural systems always move away from equilibrium as they seek innovation. Innovation is the only way they can survive—they must adapt.

What's more, "We now know that far from equilibrium, new types of structures may originate spontaneously. In far-from-equilibrium conditions we may have transformation from disorder, from thermal chaos, into order" (Prigogine & Stengers, 1984, p. 307). These two chemists and physicists were explaining that what might appear to be disorder or chaos, really has an underlying order. What the observer needs to do is allow for the order to appear. Margaret Wheatley (1994a, p. 21) explained, "As chaos theory shows, if we look at such a system long enough and with the perspective of time, it always demonstrates its inherent orderliness." Again, what might appear to be disorder is really a profound order. We humans only are able to see a small part of the system in terms of time and space. We do not see the system working in its entirety. We are not trained to do so, nor do we take the time to do so.

Nonequilibrium is actually a source of order. As Prigogine and Stengers (1984) so eloquently stated:

> In many cases it is difficult to disentangle the meaning of words such as "order" and "chaos." Is a tropical forest an ordered or a chaotic system? The history of any particular animal species will appear very contingent, dependent on other species and on environmental accidents. Nevertheless, the feeling persists that, as such, the overall pattern of a tropical forest, as represented, for instance, by the diversity of species, corresponds to the very archetype of order. (p.169)

The science of complexity has taken the next logical step beyond chaos theory. This science talks about interweaving relationships and networks, and about equilibrium as a sign of death. While the science of complexity may not yet be considered a cogent theory, the research in this broad field is very intriguing. The Santa Fe Institute in New Mexico is a fluid think-tank of some of the most brilliant minds in the world in physics, in economics, in politics, and in other fields. The scientists in the social fields know that their sciences cannot be reduced to simple linear formulas as done in the past. They know that real life is far too complex for such simplistic thinking. In his writings of real-life application of the science of complexity, Michael Waldrop (1992, p. 11) explained, "These complex, self-organizing systems are *adaptive* [emphasis in original]. . . . Species evolve for better survival in a changing environment—and so do corporations and industries." In the words of financial columnist and analyst Lauren Rudd (2001), "I firmly believe day-to-day movements on Wall Street are random and therefore unpredictable" (C2). Economic professor at Stanford University Brian Arthur extrapolated on this natural concept as reported by Waldrop (1992):

> Conventional economics, the kind he'd been taught in school, was about as far from this vision of complexity as you could imagine. Theoretical economists endlessly talked about the stability of the marketplace, and the balance of supply and demand. They transcribed the concept of mathematical equations and proved theorems about it. . . . But Arthur had embraced instability. . . . Like it or not, the market-place isn't stable. The *world* [emphasis in original] isn't stable. It's full of evolution, upheaval, and surprise. (p. 17)

The Santa Fe Institute has closely analyzed the science of complexity and the lessons that can be learned from chemistry, quantum physics, and molecular biology and how these lessons can be applied to complex organizations and systems. Molecular biologist Horace Freeland Judson posited, "The real economy was not a machine but a kind of living system, with all the spontaneity and complexity . . . in the world of molecular biology" (Waldrop, 1992, p. 31). Waldrop went on to cite the work of John Holland, computer scientist at the University of Michigan. In Waldrop's words:

> Holland started by pointing out that the economy is an example of "complex adaptive systems." In the natural world systems include brains, immune systems, ecologies, cells, developing embryos, and ant colonies. In the human world, they included cultural and social systems such as political parties or scientific communities. (p. 145)

Again, Waldrop (1992) reported on the scientific work of scientists — this time of Los Alamos physicist Doyne Farmer who talked of how the former Soviet Union changed at the edge of chaos as did the big three auto industries because of the competition coming from Japan. Farmer stated, "Common sense, not to mention recent political experience, suggests that healthy economies and healthy societies alike have to keep order and chaos in balance. . . . They leave plenty of room for creativity, change, and response to new conditions" (p. 294). Clearly, administrators choosing to tightly control their organizations in tough times may actually be squeezing the life out of their systems — a very ironic twist.

Waldrop shared one final real-life example of complexity science in action. "In the fossil record, says [biologist Stuart Kauffman of the University of Pennsylvania], this process would show up as long periods of stasis followed by bursts of evolutionary change — exactly the kind of 'punctuated equilibrium' that many paleontologists, notably Stephen J. Gould, and Niles Eldridge, claim that they do see in the record" (1992, p. 308).

There are two primary lessons we can take from chaos theory and the science of complexity back to the people in our organizations. First, people need to be patient when things *appear* to be chaotic. We need to take the time to let patterns develop, and to look over the entire system for patterns or themes in terms of space and time. The term "space" refers to the entire organization. We must look beyond our own departments or silos to see the interconnections and relationships. The term "time" refers to taking more than the typical snapshot of time in which we make our observations. That's why so much of what we see appears to be chaotic. A glimpse of nearly anything can appear chaotic. But, over time, patterns or themes tend to emerge and show themselves. So, if we look at the system over space and time, we are more likely to better understand the order out of chaos. "The very essence of living passionately is change. Life without change would soon result in death. Change is something to embrace, to invite, to zestfully seek" (Batten, 1998, p. 45). In a somewhat different tangent, Stephen Covey embraces what appears to be chaos. He wrote (1990, p. 265), "As a teacher, I have come to believe that many truly great classes teeter on the edge of chaos. There are times when neither the teacher nor the student knows for sure what's going to happen." The realization that chaos is everywhere "has begun to change the way business executives make decisions about insurance, the way astronomers look at the solar system, the way political theorists talk about the stresses leading to armed conflict," (Gleick, 1987, p. 5).

The second lesson from chaos theory and the science of complexity is no less important. "A small fluctuation may start an entirely new evolution that will drastically change the whole behavior of the macroscopic system. The analogy with social phenomena . . . is inescapable" (Prigogine & Stengers, 1984, p. 14). That is to say that the most apparently insignificant issues can create major changes. In scientific terms, quantum brain model theorist Giuseppe Vitiello (1995) posited, "Even very weak perturbations may drive the system through its macroscopic configurations," (p. 390). In terms of human organizations, one person can indeed make an enormous impact. This idea will be expanded upon in the next section. Much of chaos theory can be extrapolated from research and experiments done in chemistry and in naturally occurring phenomena. To better illustrate some of these ideas, let us now turn our attention to some of this more recent work.

DISSIPATIVE STRUCTURES AND CHEMICAL CLOCKS

Dissipative structures evolve within open systems. As Alvin Toffler wrote in the forward to Prigogine's and Stenger's book (1984):

> While some parts of the universe may operate like machines, these are closed systems, and closed systems, at best, form only a small part of the

physical universe. Most phenomenon of interest to us are, in fact, *open* [emphasis in original] systems, exchanging energy or matter (and, one might add, information) with their environment. Surely biological and social systems are open, which means that the attempt to understand them in mechanistic terms is doomed to failure. This suggests, moreover, that most of reality, instead of being orderly, stable, and equilibrial, is seething and bubbling with change, disorder, and process. (p. xv)

Therefore, open systems can only survive when they change. And, since human systems and organizations are open systems, change is crucial to their survival. We must allow for disorder and apparent chaos to work. Dissipative structures, as we shall soon see, emerge from open systems and can continue to live only through change. These systems actively seek change.

The term "dissipative structures" was innovated by Ilya Prigogine. It refers to the concept that open systems maintain features of both change and stability—another example of duality in nature. In fact, change is what allows stability. In other words, order does indeed come out of chaos. In order to survive, a natural system leaps into an apparent chaos. In complexity sciences, the fine line between order/equilibrium and chaos is where change and renewed life occurs. Nobel laureate Ilya Prigogine himself and Isabelle Stengers (1984) wrote:

One of the most interesting aspects of dissipative structures is their coherence. The system behaves as a whole, as if it were the site of long-range forces. In spite of the fact that interactions of molecules do not exceed a range of some 10(-8)cm, the system is structured as though each molecule were "informed" about the overall state of the system. (p. 171)

But before Prigogine studied the more complex systems of living organisms, he developed his theory of dissipative structures by learning of the "Benard instability," named after the French physicist Henri Benard. (The next two paragraphs contain a brief description of the Benard instability, borrowed directly from Fritjof Capra's *The Web of Life* [1996, pp. 86–87].)

Henri Benard discovered that the heating of a thin layer of liquid may result in strangely ordered structures. When the liquid is uniformly heated below, a constant heat flux is established, moving from the bottom to the top. The liquid itself remains at rest, and the heat is transferred by conduction alone. However, when the temperature difference between the top and bottom surfaces reaches a certain critical value, the heat flux is replaced by heat convection, in which the heat is transferred by the coherent motion of large numbers of molecules.

At this point a very striking ordered pattern of hexagonal ("honeycomb") cells appears, in which hot liquid rises through the center of the cells, while the cooler liquid descends to the bottom along the cell walls. Prigogine's detailed analysis of these "Benard cells" showed that as the system moves farther away from equilibrium (that is, from a state with uniform temperature throughout the liquid), it reaches a critical point of instability, at which the ordered hexagonal pattern emerges. (See figure 4.2.)

What Benard, Prigogine and Stengers, and Capra showed us is that while open systems may appear to be disorganized, there is some underlying organization and communication going on. We just can't see it. As the system moves further and further away from equilibrium or stability, it will finally reach a point of coherence and newfound stability. Again, as with the inherent communication of molecules at macroscopic distances as described by quantum physicists in the last chapter, communication is critical to open systems as described by chemists. (The reader is reminded of Bell's Theorem, or nonlocal causality where two molecules are separated at long distances, but are somehow able to communicate instantaneously over time and space.) Somehow, there is communication among these interrelated parts. Or, perhaps they are not as separate as they appear.

Ilya Prigogine alluded to another naturally occurring example of dissipative structures in open systems. Again, we turn to Fritjof Capra for his excellent description—in the next several paragraphs—of the vortex funnel in *The Web of Life* (1996, pp. 169–170).

One of the simplest structures of this kind is a vortex in flowing water—for example, a whirlpool in a bathtub. Water continuously flows

 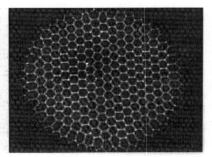

Figure 4.2   Benard Cells

through the vortex, yet its characteristic shape, the well-known spirals and narrowing funnel, remains remarkably stable. It is a dissipative structure.

Closer examination of the origin and progression of such a vortex reveals a series of rather complex phenomena. Imagine a bathtub with shallow, motionless water. When the drain is opened, the water begins to run out, flowing radially toward the drain and speeding up as it approaches the hole under the accelerating force of gravity. Thus a smooth uniform flow is established. The flow does not remain in this smooth state for long, however. Tiny irregularities in the water movement, movements of the air at the water's surface, and irregularities in the drainpipe will cause a little more water to approach the drain on one side than the other, and thus a whirling, rotary motion is introduced into the flow.

As the water particles are dragged down toward the drain, both their radial and rotational velocities increase. They speed up radially because of the accelerating force of gravity, and they pick up rotational speed as the radius of their rotation decreases, like a skater pulling in her arms during a pirouette. As a result, the water particles move downward in spirals, forming a narrowing tube of flow lines, known as a vortex tube.

Because the basic flow is still radially inward, the vortex tube is continually squeezed by the water pressing against it from all sides. This pressure decreases its radius and intensifies the rotation further. Using Prigogine's language, we can say that the rotation introduces an instability into the initial uniform flow. The force of gravity, the water pressure, and the constantly diminishing radius of the vortex tube all combine to accelerate the whirling motion to ever-increasing speeds.

However, this continuing acceleration ends not in catastrophe but in a new stable state. At a certain rotational speed, centrifugal forces come into play that push the water radially away from the drain. Thus the water surface above the drain develops a depression, which quickly turns into a funnel. Eventually a miniature tornado of air forms inside this funnel, creating highly complex and nonlinear structures, ripples, waves, and eddies—on the water surface inside the vortex.

In the end the force of gravity pulling the water down the drain and the water pressure pushing outward balance each other and result in a stable state, in which gravity maintains the flow of energy at the larger scale, and friction dissipates some of its smaller scales. The acting forces are now interlinked in self-balancing feedback loops that give great stability to the vortex structure as a whole. (See figure 4.3.)

Figure 4.3   Vortex

Again, we are shown that somehow, the seemingly disorganized and chaotic system self-organizes and a new order comes into existence. The message from dissipative structures is clear. As Margaret Wheatley (1994a) so eloquently put it:

> Dissipative structures demonstrate that *disorder* can be a source of *order*, and that most growth is found in disequilibrium, not in balance. The things we fear most in organizations—fluctuations, disturbances, imbalances—need not be signs of an impending disorder that will destroy us. Instead, fluctuations are the primary source of creativity. (p. 20)

Chemical clocks prove to be another amazing dissipative structure phenomenon that provide intriguing insights into systems. For one final time we turn, in the next two paragraphs, to Fritjof Capra's *Web of Life* (1996, p. 88) for this excellent description.

> [Chemical clocks show] reactions far from equilibrium, which produce very striking periodic oscillations. For example, if there are two kinds of molecules in the reaction, one "red" and one "blue," the system will be all blue at a certain point; then change its color abruptly to red; then

again to blue; and so on at regular intervals—like clockwork. Different experimental conditions may also produce waves of chemical activity.

To change all at once, the chemical system has to act as a whole, producing a high degree of order through the coherent activity of billions of molecules. Prigogine and his colleagues discovered that, as in the Benard convection, this coherent behavior emerges spontaneously at critical points of instability far from equilibrium.

Prigogine (Prigogine & Stengers, 1984, p. 168) himself wrote that, "In chemistry the relation between order and chaos appears highly complex: successive regimes of ordered (oscillatory) situations follow regimes of chaotic behavior." Again, as with quantum physic's nonlocal causality and as with chemistry's dissipative structures, molecules show a sense of relationships and corresponding communication that seems counterintuitive to our Western linear minds. Each molecule appears to know what the others are doing. Again, in Prigogine's own words (Prigogine & Stengers, 1984):

> Particles separated by macroscopic distances become linked. Local events have repercussions throughout the whole system. . . . Nonequilibrium is a source of order. Here the situation is especially clear. At equilibrium molecules behave as essentially independent entities; they ignore one another. We would like to call them "hypnons," "sleepwalkers." Though each of them may be as complex as we like, they ignore one another. However, nonequilibrium wakes them up and introduces a coherence quite foreign to equilibrium. (p. 180)

Gleick (1987) described the work of biologist Robert May who saw oscillating behavior in nature:

> As May looked at more and more biological systems throughout the prism of simple chaotic models, he continued to see results that violated the standard intuition of practitioners. In epidemiology, for example, it was well known that epidemics tend to come in cycles, regular or irregular. Measles, polio, rubella—all rise and fall in frequency. May realized that the oscillations could be reproduced by a nonlinear model and he wondered what would happen if such a system received a sudden kick— a perturbation of the kind that might correspond to a program of inoculation. Naive intuition suggests that the system will change smoothly in the desired direction. But actually, May found, huge oscillations are likely to begin. Even if the long-term trend was turned solidly downward, the path to a new equilibrium would be interrupted by surprising

peaks. In fact, in data from real programs, such as a campaign to wipe
out rubella in Britain, doctors had seen oscillations just like those pre-
dicted by May's model. Yet any health official, seeing a sharp short-term
rise in rubella or gonorrhea, would assume that the inoculation program
had failed. (p. 79)

The message from these experiments and from nature itself must be
clear to educational leaders. Communication is central to the revital-
ization and survival of open systems. Furthermore, what might appear
to be chaos, is either order that we have not taken the time or breadth
of view to see, or is part of the process of the system attempting to re-
new itself. We need to allow this process to occur.

Still, other new sciences and old sciences with new knowledge bring
us even more insights, as well. The following section will briefly touch
upon what we are learning today.

FIELDS, FORCES, FRACTALS, AND OTHER FUNNY THINGS

Ancient Eastern philosophers have intuited a very special sense of the
forces acting throughout nature. Confucian philosopher Nakae Toju of
Japan believed, "There emerges a unique sense of reverence for this nu-
minous force, which is simultaneously behind and within the universe.
This ground of being and cause of life is seen as the source of the unity
of life" (Tucker, 1995, p. 352). Mihaly Csikszentmihalyi (1990) veri-
fied that we often feel such forces when we are truly focused in a flow-
state of concentration. For example,

> In a chess tournament, players whose attention has been riveted, for
> hours, to the logical battle on the board claim that they feel as if they
> have been merged into a powerful "field of force" clashing with other
> forces in some nonmaterial dimension of existence. (p. 64)

We all innately feel these forces and strange fields, but we ignore
them or dispel them for lack of scientific proof. However, modern scientists have made discoveries that also support this notion of forces.

Each of us remembers studying in high school gravitational, mag-
netic, and electromagnetic force fields. But there are other scientific
forces and fields that are very powerful and intriguing, too.

One of the most amazing concepts is morphogenic fields as developed by Rupert Sheldrake. Morphogenic fields, or form-generating

fields, describe species memory. In other words, memory is handed down from one generation to the next. While this might seem implausible, real examples help to clarify. Gary Schwartz and Linda Russek tell of an actual experiment carried out by Rupert Sheldrake. Schwartz and Russek reported this experiment in their book *The Living Energy Universe* (1999, pp. 123–125). To paraphrase their description, Sheldrake did an experiment on national television in Britain. Using controlled procedures, Sheldrake showed a never-before-seen embedded picture to the national television-viewing audience. Embedded pictures are those apparently chaotic pictures we have stared at for long moments to see the real picture behind the lines. All of a sudden the picture seems to jump out at us, and then we are always able to see the picture behind the lines. Sheldrake randomly selected one of four embedded pictures and showed it to the television audience. Remember, these pictures had never been seen before except by their artist-creator. Sheldrake then took all four embedded pictures to people all around the world—these people did not see the television program. He showed all four photos to these people. Amazingly, they were able to find the picture in the embedded photo shown to the British national audience quicker than the three that had not been viewed previously. He replicated this same type of experiment in Germany, with similar results. These experiments are believed to be indicative of morphogenic fields. These memories or information "live" in fields across space and time, much like gravitational fields or electromagnetic fields. Remarkably, people in countries closer to the original television viewing (countries surrounding Britain or Germany, as the case may be) were able to observe the embedded picture quicker than people from countries further away. In other words, the morphogenic fields become weaker and weaker with distance.

You may have heard of an example where a pet squirrel that had never seen another animal was allowed to hop along the ground in a city park. A rabbit entered the scene and the squirrel thought nothing of it. Later, a cat entered the scene and the squirrel scampered for cover. This squirrel had never seen a cat before, so it did not know from past experience that it could be in danger. This event could not be explained away due to the innate worrisome nature of squirrels, as the squirrel did not scamper away from the rabbit. The concept of morphogenic fields would explain that the squirrel's ancestors had learned about the dangers of cats or catlike creatures, and the memories were passed on through genetics to the following generations.

Still another example is the case where scientists, in a laboratory setting, experimented with morphogenic fields. In this particular case, the
scientists placed a nest of duck eggs within an enclosed area. (See figure 4.4.) Above the enclosure hung a rotating mobile with a single figure. The mobile could spin either in a clockwise or counterclockwise
direction. Looking from below at this figure, from one direction it
looked like an adult duck's head—conceivably that of a mother duck.
Looking up at this figure from the other direction, it looked more like
a hawk in flight. After the eggs had hatched, the scientists put the mobile in motion. At first, the mobile was spun in the direction whereby
the figure looked like a head of a mother duck. The ducklings were
calm and went about their business. However, the mobile was then put
in motion in the other direction—where it looked like a hawk in flight.
The little ducklings responded in a panic and scattered about the enclosure. Again, the concept of morphogenic fields would explain this as
an example where past generations of ducks passed this experiential
knowledge through their genes to the succeeding generations.

Duck

Hawk

**Figure 4.4   Morphogenic Field
Example**

These examples of morphogenic fields show us that somehow learning is passed down from generation to generation. Even more so, learning becomes more efficient and quicker for subsequent generations (Wheatley, 1994a, p. 51). Holistic psychiatrist Carl Jung also saw fields theory in his synchronistic work. Leonard Shlain (1998) explained:

> Jung was the first man of science to propose that we are all born with an extensive foreknowledge of the world. Previously, Western rationalists had accepted with few caveats Locke's concept of a newborn's brain as a *tabula rasa,* a clean slate upon which culture could write. Jung disagreed. He named his ancient knowing the "Collective Unconscious" and envisioned it as an inherited extra-corporeal net holding bits of experience filtered down through the consciousness of our forebears, both human and non-human. (p. 396)

Each of us has seen other natural examples of other fields. We have seen how an enormous flock of birds instinctively move together as if by remote control. We see how they undulate and turn in unison in different directions, *as if by some invisible force*, unconsciously organizing themselves into a flock (Waldrop, 1992, p. 111). We have seen other such examples of schools of fish moving together, weaving back and forth in unison as they feed or as they escape from a predator. Wheatley (1994a) goes on to discuss the significance of fields theories:

> Fields encourage us to think of a universe that more closely resembles an ocean, filled with interpenetrating influences and invisible structures that connect. . . . In the field world, there are potentials for action everywhere, anywhere two fields meet. (p. 51)

It would seem that fields theories show us how information and knowledge can actually live, or at least take on a life of its own. "Quantum phenomena provide *prima facie* evidence that information gets around in ways that do not conform to classical ideas. Thus, the idea that information is transferred superliminally is *a priori*, is not unreasonable" (Zukav, 1980, p. 295). Again, we find a common thread of relationships and interconnectedness in life. These relationships and sharing of information cannot be controlled, rather they happen naturally in a very dynamic way.

The relatively new and fascinating science of fractals again captivates the mind as we peer into a more and more microscopic world. Scientists have been able to create computerized geometric images from very simple nonlinear equations that are fed back upon themselves, over and over. What results is a beautiful array of unique patterns. (See figures 4.5 through 4.9.) Since one cannot predict or control what the fractal will look like, no two fractals are alike. But these beautiful fractals do not occur only on the computer screen. Nature is replete with the beauty of fractals. The first example fractal neophytes learn of is the typical fern plant. Other examples include cauliflower, clouds, mountain ranges, and even our brains (Amoroso & Martin, 1995). When the observer studies one of these objects, he or she notices a pattern in the shape of the leaf or of the cloud. If one then looks even closer and closer, these same patterns continually appear over and over again at ever increasing microscopic levels. One can never seem to see the end. It reminds one of walking into a hall of mirrors where two mirrors are facing one another and the same im-

Figure 4.5   Fractal of a Fern Created on a Computer
Source: McGuire, M. (1991). An eye for fractals: A graphic and photographic essay. New York: Addison-Wesley Publishing.

Figure 4.6   Naturally Occurring Fractal—An Oak Tree
Source: McGuire, M. (1991). An eye for fractals: A graphic and pho-
tographic essay. New York: Addison-Wesley Publishing.

Figure 4.7   Fractal Example of a Mandelbrot Set
Source: Peitgen, H., & Richter, P. (1986). The beauty of fractals:
Images of Complex Dynamical Systems. Heidelberg, Germany:
Springer-Verlag.

Figure 4.8   Another Fractal Example of a Mandelbrot Set
Source: Peitgen, H., & Richter, P. (1986). The beauty of fractals: Images of Complex Dynamical Systems. Heidelberg, Germany: Springer-Verlag.

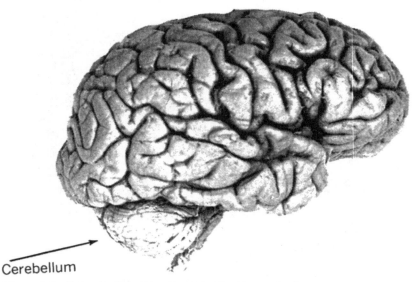

Cerebellum

Figure 4.9   Naturally Occurring Fractal—The Human Brain
Source: McConnell, J. (1980). Understanding Human Behavior. New York: Holt, Rinehart, and Winston.

ages continually reflect back upon one another at ever decreasing sizes. Gleick (1987) noted:

> Clouds are not spheres, Mandelbrot is fond of saying. Mountains are not cones. Lightning does not travel in a straight line. The new geometry mirrors a universe that is rough, not rounded, scabrous, not smooth. It is a geometry of the pitted, pocked, and broken up, the twisted, tangled, and intertwined. The understanding of nature's complexity awaited a suspicion that the complexity was not just random, not just an accident. . . . Mandelbrot's work made a claim about the world, and the claim was that such odd shapes carry meaning. The pits and tangles are more than blemishes distorting the classic shapes of Euclidian geometry. They are often the keys to the essence of a thing. (p. 94)

The study of fractals tells us that nature is filled with patterns and not simple, separate cause-and-effect relationships. "A fractal curve implies an organizing structure that lies hidden among the hideous complication of such shapes" (Gleick, 1987, p. 114). When observing nature and human dynamic systems, we must purposefully seek out patterns and recurring themes. We need to look at the bigger picture over time and space. The more we quantify, the further we get away from the big picture. It becomes impossible for us to see patterns and themes. In terms of lessons to be learned for those working in organizations, Margaret Wheatley (1994a) posited:

> Fractals suggest the futility of searching for ever finer measures of discrete parts of the system. There is never a satisfying end to this reductionist search, never an end point where we finally know everything about even one part of the system. (p. 129)

It would appear that the lesson from fractals is that we may never be able to observe something at its most fundamental point. Each observation shows more of the same thing. Looking ever deeper only shows more of the same. In fact, looking in ever more detail is the wrong direction. We need to step back and broaden our view over time and space. We need to see the entire organization, not individual departments or classrooms. We need to look for patterns or recurring themes that happen month after month, and year after year. Searching for ever finer detail takes us further and further away from anything meaningful.

Before this chapter concludes, it is worthwhile to take a look at a couple of phenomena from the study of ecology and see what lessons we can take from them. Fritjof Capra cited an amazing example of how an aggregation of thousands of single cell creatures can communicate and come together to work as a single system for their survival. (The following paragraph is such an example borrowed from Capra's 1996, *The Web of Life*, pp. 246–247).

> A spectacular example of such aggregation is the slime mold, an organism that is macroscopic but is technically a protist. [See figure 4.10.] A slime mold has a complex life cycle involving a mobile (animal-like) and an immobile (plant-like) phase. In the animal-like phase it starts out as a multitude of single cells, commonly found in forests under rotting logs and damp leaves, where they feed on other microorganisms and decaying vegetation. The cells often eat so much and divide so rapidly that they deplete the entire food supply in their environment. When this happens they aggregate into a cohesive mass of thousands of cells, resembling a slug and capable of creeping across the forest floor in amoeba-like movements. When it has found a new source of food, the mold enters its plantlike phase, developing a stalk with a fruiting body and looking very much like a fungus. Finally, the fruit capsule bursts, shooting thousands of dry spores from which new individual cells are born, to move about independently in the search for food, starting a new cycle of life.

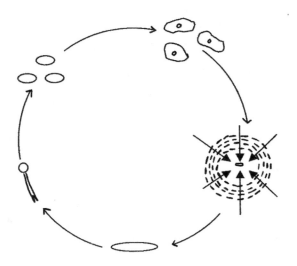

Figure 4.10   Slime Mold Cycle

In other words, somehow these separate individuals mysteriously communicate and come together simultaneously. They self-organize in order to survive.

Again, we learn that communication, at the macroscopic level, is central to the life of the system. Peter Senge (1996) explained the significance of this message as it relates to human organizations:

> "Gradually, I have come to see a whole new model for my role as a CEO," says Shell Oil's Phil Carroll. "Perhaps my real job is to be the *ecologist for the organization* [emphasis in original]. We must learn how to see the company as a living system and to see it as a system within the context of the larger systems of which it is a part." (p. 53)

POINTS TO PONDER

1. What is Leslie doing that would be considered classical leadership?
2. How could she change these things in order to incorporate the lessons from quantum physics and the other new sciences?
3. What is Leslie doing that is following lessons from quantum physics and the other new sciences?
4. Describe chaos theory. What do we learn from it?
5. Describe dissipative structures. What do we learn from them?
6. Describe fractals. What do we learn from them?
7. How can you apply any of these ideas to the issue you addressed in the last chapter?

CHAPTER 5

Implications for Leadership

To be responsible inventors and discoverers, though, we need the courage to let go of the old world, to relinquish most of what we have cherished, to abandon our interpretations about what does and doesn't work. As Einstein is often quoted as saying: "No problem can be solved from the same consciousness that created it. We must learn to see the world anew.

—Wheatley, 1994a, p. 5

LESLIE'S LAMENT

Leslie and Cindy got together for a homemade Tex-Mex dinner on Sunday. While they were frying up the beans and the meat, Cindy told Leslie, "There is a rumor circulating that our firm is to be sold to another larger umbrella group. It's got all of us concerned, Les."

"Oh, I'm sorry to hear that, Cindy. What is that going to mean for your job? Will you still work there?"

"I don't think I'll have any problems in that respect," bemoaned Cindy. "The company that is buying us wants us to restructure our organizational chart. Our new CEO, if this happens, has a reputation for making radical changes. He says the only way an organization can live today is to position itself to be able to respond to rapid change. We'll find out on Monday what happens."

"Man, I'm glad I'm in public education," Leslie said in a concerned voice. "We would never get bought out and have to make such drastic changes."

Cindy looked at her sister as if to say, "Don't be so sure." Leslie felt uneasy. Cindy finally said, "Let's sit down and eat and forget about work for awhile."

After dinner, Leslie and Cindy cleared the table and began the dishes. Cindy questioned Leslie, "How did your faculty meeting go?"

"I'm so glad you asked. I've been waiting to tell you all evening. The meeting started off very, very slowly. I thought the timing was bad or that I wasn't prepared. But, by the end of the meeting we had some healthy dialogue, and we got together a committee to explore supervision and evaluation. I think we might make some good progress. Let's say, 'I'm hopeful.'"

"What are the concerns? Did they have any good ideas?" Cindy asked.

Leslie jumped in excitedly, "It's very clear they don't want to evaluate each other—at least not in the traditional sense. They're also concerned about having enough time to supervise one another. That will ultimately be the biggest issue, I think. They also don't know how to supervise; so they want some ideas. I don't know too much else—that will probably come from our meeting Wednesday morning."

"I wish you guys the best of luck, Leslie," Cindy proclaimed as she put away the dishes. "I wish I could be a fly on the wall of your office on Wednesday."

With a loving hug, they called it an evening. "Have fun at work, Leslie," Cindy said.

"I'll call you tomorrow night to see what you learned about your corporation, okay. You take care of yourself and keep your chin up," chirped Leslie.

As promised, Leslie called Cindy on Monday night. "What's the verdict, hon?"

"Just like we thought—we got sold out. But I think it might be a good move. We met the new CEO, and he has a lot of energy, but I also get a sense that he is friendly and caring. This might just be what we need," Cindy said.

"Well, good, I think. I wish you the best of luck. Did he show you your new organizational chart?" inquired Leslie.

"No, interestingly. He wants the entire management team to attend a Thursday-Friday seminar at the Vista Resort at the end of the week. He's bringing in some leadership gurus with backgrounds in science. I'm a little skeptical, no, really skeptical. But, a couple of days away from the office should be great."

"That sounds like fun. I love science, and I think it would be a blast! I don't see the connection of science to your work, but I would love it!" exclaimed Leslie.

"OK, you're in!"

"Wh-what do you mean? I can't go. I don't work at your company," fretted Leslie.

"Oh, of course you can go. You will be my guest. Besides, you'd add another neat perspective to the group. I'll double-check tomorrow."

Leslie was mad at herself for opening her big mouth, but knew she couldn't back out now. "OK, sounds like a plan."

Leslie got to work early on Wednesday. She wanted to make sure she was ready to meet with her supervision and evaluation committee. As she was getting out the policy manual and principal handbook for teacher supervision and evaluation, the committee members began to stroll in with freshly poured coffee.

Vicki Gibson began, "My great idea of meeting sounded greater the other afternoon than it does now. This is too early to hold a meeting."

Leslie gave a half-hearted laugh only because she was feeling the same way somehow. "Where would you like to begin?"

Since there was complete silence, Leslie looked directly at Mary Thompson and asked, "Mary, I observed you last week. How could I be more meaningful to you as a supervisor?"

Mary didn't know what to say, so she said, "I don't know what to say. Perhaps we should go back to the beginning. What is the purpose of teacher supervision?"

"That really gets to the crux of the issue, Mary," Leslie said. "What do you guys think?"

Mike Tippler jumped in, "I think it's time for another cup of coffee. But seriously, there has to be some level of accountability in all of this. I mean, the principal has to be able to say which teachers are cutting it and which ones don't belong in the profession. And they should put this in writing."

"I agree with you completely, Mike," Leslie said. "However, I think that is the role of evaluation. Teachers are evaluated at how well they are doing their jobs, and whether or not they get to keep their jobs or need intensive assistance. Do you guys think that sounds correct?"

Hannah interjected, "For now that sounds good. I'd have to think about it some more, so don't hold me to it. But in order for us to get back on track, I'll agree. So, what is the purpose of supervision?"

Mike vaulted right back in, "All right, if evaluation is the principal's role for accountability purposes, then supervision should be more like growth-oriented—more like staff development. Wait, that doesn't sound right. I mean like instructional development. I'm trying to make the point that supervision should be to help teachers become better teachers. I guess that could even mean stuff outside the classroom, outside of instruction—like assessment and curriculum work. What do you think, Mary?"

"To be honest, I think you're right on, Mike. I think that we all could use another set of eyes to help us look at what we're doing in the classroom. I know that I'm focusing on instruction right now, but that's the most important part. And, the extra set of eyes doesn't have to be the principal's eyes. I do think we could observe one another. Leslie, if we do observe one another, does that mean we have to put the observation in writing?"

"I haven't ever considered that question before," Leslie replied. "Obviously, the evaluation report has to be put in writing—that goes in your personnel file. I don't know about . . . I'm talking out loud now, so give me a second. I know that each teacher in the cycle needs to be observed three times a year. And, I don't think the teachers want to do that if they have to put the report in writing—even if it's just an observation—that goes into your personnel files. Maybe, just maybe, I can still be the one to do the three annual observations—for accountability purposes—but teachers can observe one another, unofficially. Nothing has to go in writing. You can choose to put it in your file, or not. I really hesitate to ask for permission from downtown. Because if they don't want me to do this approach, then we have to go with what they say. I like to go with the saying, 'Do what you want and ask for forgiveness later.' I say we just go with it."

While Leslie began feeling kind of like a maverick, Hannah chimed in, "I'm not sure we want to do this. I don't want to start doing something and then be told we can't do it."

"Lighten up, Hannah," Mike burst in. "What are they going to do? Send us to Lincoln School? We're not saying anyone has to do this. It's just open to them on a voluntary basis. Maybe we can pilot this, huh, Vicki?"

"What good is it if Leslie still has to observe us? I mean, now we could be getting observed six or more times," Vicki said incredulously.

"That's not necessarily so," Mary Thompson stated. Mary sat for a moment mulling over her position. "I share your concern. It does seem to be somewhat of a waste of time. Still, Leslie can fill the bureaucratic function, and we can provide the meaningful growth-related function." Sensing she'd diss'd Leslie, Mary continued, "I'm not saying that you can only play a bureaucratic role, Leslie. You can also be a growth-oriented observer. In areas where you have special expertise or experience—like English, you might be the most appropriate one."

Everyone felt a sense of relief at how deftly Mary got herself out of that jam. Vicki joined back in, "I see. I see. We can just open this idea up to people who are interested. We really won't be changing anything, at least not in terms of dropping any current requirements. Leslie will still do her regular observations and end-of-the-year evaluations. We teachers can then go into each other's rooms and observe each other. But, why would I want to do that?"

"For professional growth—to become a better teacher," Mike said.

"Can you give me an example?" Vicki rejoined.

Mary said, "Sure. Let's say that Lawrence, your new social studies teacher colleague, wants to know if he is doing a good job with higher-level questioning. Now, while Leslie could come in and give some feedback, Lawrence asks you to observe him. He asks you because you have taught social studies for the past five years. You know the tricks and whether the kids are getting it, just by watching how they react."

Mike quickly interrupted, "Or, you could have me come in to observe to see if the way you are teaching the kids some culture's dance is the correct way or not."

Vicki looked at Mike quizzically, but said, "Mary, I gotcha."

Hannah said, "Okay, I've got an idea; this all sounds good. Why doesn't each of us think more about this and maybe even try out an observation. We can meet next week—same time and place and see how we've done."

Leslie concluded, "This sounds great. Let's give it a try."

The next day, a chilly and rainy Thursday morning, Cindy and Leslie arrived at the Vista Resort. Leslie was not the only noncorporation person in attendance. Cindy's new CEO also had invited the president of the Britton Chamber of Commerce, the mayor, and the president of the local university. Likewise, a couple of Cindy's colleagues brought along spouses and friends. All told, there were twenty-eight people in attendance.

The room was arranged with tables in a big circle. The circle was actually about four feet short of being completely enclosed; enough room was allowed for someone to easily walk among the tables. The chairs were very comfortable. They were the kind of office chairs with plenty of cushioning, small wheels, and backs that could be adjusted. Each table had plenty of water, and there were snacks, sodas, and juices in the back of the room. The front of the room had a portable marker board and several flip charts. The conference room itself had windows on three sides. Two of the sides looked out into serene woods, while the third side looked over a very large pond. Leslie thought to herself, "Now I know how the other half lives. It sure would be nice to have our inservices out here."

Everyone was casually dressed—nobody looked like a consultant or CEO. A few minutes after 8:00, Cindy's CEO—Bernard—welcomed everyone with warmth and excitement. Bernard then introduced the two "leadership colleagues"—Woodrow and Marva. Woodrow had retired from his former job as an executive vice president of a Japanese automobile company—in charge of foreign markets. Prior to that, he held the same position at an American automobile company, but left because he "needed something more rewarding" in his life. Marva was a university physicist who was gradually leaving the classroom and spending more and more time writing and traveling to similar workshops.

Woodrow began by asking everyone to write a personal list of complaints they had about their organizational structure and about their own jobs. After sharing their issues and concerns, they narrowed the group list down to: too much bureaucracy, communication problems, turfism, slow reaction/unresponsive to change, and not enough time. (Leslie wanted to add, "school boards' and administrators' snapshot approach to assessment," but she didn't want to bring in education at this point.) Woodrow said the list would be virtually identical to the list that could be compiled at any organization. He went on to give a brief history of why organizations exist today the way they do, and why they wouldn't be able to survive the twenty-first century if they didn't learn to evolve. Leslie wrote down two books that he recommended: Patrick Dolan's *Restructuring Our Schools: A Primer on Systemic Change,* and Peter Block's *Stewardship: Choosing Service Over Self-interest.* Woodrow also mentioned how his life fairly well mirrored that of Joseph Jaworski in *Synchronicity: The Inner Path of Leadership.*

Woodrow then said, "We'll be taking a break in about fifteen minutes. But first, I want to express my point very clearly. Our society has taken the lessons we learn from science very seriously. We have developed our organizations, our military, our factories, and our schools from what we have learned in the sciences. We have applied these lessons to how we work, how we teach, and how we work with one another. The science has not been wrong! Our application of the sciences into the workplace often has been wrong! We have benefited greatly from Newtonian physics, but we have misapplied the science to our work lives. However, we are learning lessons from the newer sciences that are a much better fit in terms of their application to our organizations. It's not that the science is the answer. But, these newer sciences do seem to support what we intuitively know about people and organizations. I think they let us know that our gut-level feelings of what is wrong with our organizations are correct. There is a different way to structure our organizations and to interact with each other." Woodrow took a deep and refreshing breath. "After the break, Marva will launch us off into these new discoveries. In fact, we'll spend the rest of the day learning about these new sciences. Tomorrow, we will create. We will create our own models for our new organizations. In other words, we'll take a look at how these lessons can be applied immediately to our work. Now let's stretch!"

During the break, Leslie and Cindy each got a juice and bagel. Cindy began, "This sounds pretty intriguing. Do you see similar concerns in the private sector to your public work?"

"Actually, I do. The more I work with people in business and in other social organizations, the more similarities I see. I do enjoy the flexibility I get as a principal. I get to meet so many people from different kinds of jobs. I was so isolated as a teacher."

Just then Cal, the president of the chamber of commerce, strolled up to Leslie and Cindy. "Good morning, Cindy. Aren't you going to introduce me to your friend?"

Biting her cheek, Cindy said, "Of course, Cal. Cal, this is my sister Leslie. She's the principal of Washington Elementary School. Leslie, this is Cal of the chamber."

Cal continued, "It's clearly my pleasure to meet you, Leslie. So, what do you girls think about all this esoteric stuff? It sounds like a pretty slick way of making five grand to me. I mean, really, it's the same old message, just warmed up in a new wrapper. Am I right, girls?"

Cindy interjected, "Well, we're only girls. So, it's too soon for us to tell." Marva called the group back to the circle. "Saved by the bell," Cindy cried to Leslie.

THE SCIENCE

We have covered a great deal of new territory in these past two chapters. It would be wise now to briefly review all the key theoretical and

experimental concepts just explored and then restate their corresponding lessons.

QUANTUM PHYSICS

Double Slit Experiment

The double slit experiment brings forth the notion of the particle-
wave duality. We have learned through our classical physics training
that light can be considered either particlelike or wavelike, but never
both at the same time. However, as you will recall, in this real-life experiment light passes through a device that can allow the light to go
through the slits as single particles or through the slits and show wavelike characteristics. Oddly enough, the measuring device has shown
that the light behaves as both individual particles and together as waves
simultaneously; hence, the particle-wave duality. Through this Principle of Complementarity, we have learned that indeed light does have
dualistic attributes. In fact, in the words of Gary Zukav (1980, p. 32),
"At the subatomic level, mass and energy change unceasingly into each
other." In other words, mass and energy are one and the same thing—
they are not separate as we have been taught. What's more, our observations limit our views or understanding of this concept. We have only
been able to set up experiments to measure one thing at a time, so we
have seen nature as a singular phenomenon. And that is the Principle of
Uncertainty. We know reality is multidimensional, but we can only observe one piece at a time. Ronald Pine (2000) explained:

> Wave-particle duality is nature's way of informing us that we have no
> right to impose our human concepts on the subatomic level. Just as Ein-
> stein had discovered that we have no right to impose our normal as-
> sumptions of space and time to all levels of reality, so quantum physics
> reveals that we have no right to our most basic thoughts about the nature
> of reality on the subatomic realm. (p. 226)

We have learned that our observations are very limited, and that the
observer actually is not separate from what is being observed. In other
words, the very act of observing alters nature. According to Zukav
(1980, p. 65), "The wave-particle duality marked the end of the 'Either-
Or' way of looking at the world. Physicists no longer could accept the
proposition that light is *either* a particle *or* a wave because they had

'proved' to themselves that it was *both*, depending on how they looked at it." Again, "Might we humans also, in some mysterious way, have both particle-like individuality and wave-like shared beings and inter-connectedness?" (Gilman, 1993, p. 11).

Schrodinger's Cat

Erwin Schrodinger created that nonsensical experiment in which he placed a cat inside a tightly sealed box. In that box the cat had a 50/50 chance to survive as there was a "diabolic device" that would dispense either food or deadly cyanide gas. The absurdity of this experiment is shown through the mathematics of the probability function. The probability function shows us that the cat is both dead and alive at the same time, that is until the moment of observation. Until something—in this case the cat—is observed, its existence is regarded as a set of probabilities.

We are reminded, as we were with the double slit experiment, that nature is dualistic or multiplistic. Nature does not exist only as we see it. Both the observer and the act of observation help to create reality. We are a part of nature, not apart from nature. We cannot separate ourselves from nature as we are part of nature. Therefore, we cannot be objective. Objectivity in nature is a facade. Life is subjective. We are more of a participator than an impartial observer.

Bell's Theorem

Bell's Theorem is also known as the Principle of Nonlocal Causality. This experiment was performed mathematically before it was done in the laboratory. What John Bell discovered was the idea that you could pair together two electrons. Once they were paired together, you could separate them at macroscopic distances. After they were separated, the experimenter/observer could change the spin of one of the electrons. In a most interesting twist, the other electron would instantaneously change its spin in a corresponding fashion even though it could not "see" the other electron. How could this be?

We are again trapped by our limited, classical thinking. It is *apparent* that the two objects are separate, but that is the trap. The two objects are not necessarily two objects, or separate. They are interconnected, or one object. "It is a quantum loophole through which physics admits the necessity of a unitary vision" (Jaworski, 1996, p. 79). Inter-connectedness and relationships are the centerpiece to this quantum world, and communication is the foundation to these relationships. There is not an observer separate from the observed. The observer and observed are linked together as part of the whole. Fritjof Capra (1996) went still further when he said:

> Living systems are integrated wholes whose properties cannot be re-duced to those of smaller parts. Their essential, or 'systemic,' properties are properties of the whole, which none of the parts have. They arise from the "organizing relations" of the parts. . . . Systemic properties are destroyed when a system is dissected into isolated elements. (p. 36)

Again, we learn of the unifying context of nature. We are not sepa-rate, we are interconnected. Isolating through measurement of individ-ual parts does not give us a better understanding of the whole. Since the whole is greater than the sum of its parts, the whole can only be un-derstood by examining the entire system in a unified fashion—over time and space.

THE OTHER NEW SCIENCES

Chaos Theory and the Science of Complexity

"In our world, complexity flourishes, and those looking to science for a general understanding of nature's habits will be better served by the laws of chaos" (Gleick, 1987, p. 308). From chaos theory we learn that systems strive to change in order to survive. Equilibrium means death. Survival requires evolution so that the system can meet the ever changing demands of the environment. As a matter of fact, as Gleick (1987, p. 314) quoted Georgia Institute of Technology physicist Joseph Ford, "Evolution is chaos with feedback." Often, what *appears* to be chaos or disorder is actually the system in the process of change. We simply have not seen the entire system or taken the opportunity to look at the system over a sufficient amount of time.

We need to sit back and let patterns develop, and to look over the en-tire system for patterns and themes in terms of time and space. We must look across the system for interconnections and relationships among departments and people. "One of the most powerful lessons from the new science called chaos is the concept that everything is totally connected to everything else in an unbroken wholeness" (Gelatt, 1995, p. 108). Furthermore, chaos theory and the butterfly effect teach us that small fluctuations, or even one person, can cause an entire system to jump into disorder and to a higher level of organization. Finally, while higher levels of organization can come from apparent chaos, disorder does not necessarily guarantee a new order. When a system moves into a far-from-equilibrium state, it eventually reaches a bifurcation point. The bifurcation point is when the system will either jump to a higher level of order, or crash into its death. However, change is the only way a system can survive. Doing everything we can to control a system— keep it in order—will guarantee the system's eventual death. In the words of Ilya Prigogine and Isabelle Stengers (1984), "Particles separated by macroscopic distances become linked. Local events have repercussions throughout the whole system. . . . Nonequilibrium is a source of order" (p. 180). Educational philosopher Parker Palmer (1998) summed up the need for chaos in organizations, "Chaos is the precondition to creativity. . . . When a leader is so fearful of chaos as not to be able to protect and nurture that arena for other people, there is deep trouble" (p. 206). We must look to stir up and welcome chaos if our organizations are to have any chance to survive.

Dissipative Structures and Chemical Clocks

Dissipative structures refer to the ability of open systems to maintain features of both change and stability, simultaneously, in order to survive. This duality of nature is an extension of chaos theory. Somehow systems, in the midst of chaos, are able to instantaneously communicate over macroscopic distances and create a new order. These systems are a coherent whole. "Prigogine's definition of open dissipative structures encompasses human social behavior, chemical reactions, and ecosystems: things whose structures are maintained by continuous flows of energy permeating them" (Tucker, 1983, p. 86).

The Benard instability experiment is an excellent example of a dissipative structure. In this actual assay, liquid is heated uniformly. Suddenly, this chaotic boiling liquid reaches its bifurcation point. The system leaps into an ordered pattern of hexagonal cells. Again, there is some type of systemic communication occurring across the system. The observer, however, cannot see it. Whirlpools show us the same kind of apparent chaos, or disorder, and subsequent communication and reorganization.

Just as the Benard instability proves to be an incredible example of dissipative structure, so too do chemical clocks. When an external force, say heat, is added to a mixture of different color molecules, the molecules will swirl about in apparent disarray. Suddenly, like clockwork, the molecules will abruptly become ordered. For example, if a mixture of red and blue molecules are placed together into a container, the mixture will turn purple. However, the mixture will all of a sudden pulsate from all red to all blue. Just as quickly as they congealed, they will fall back into apparent disarray, and then again reorganize.

As is the message with all dissipative structures, we learn that the system is able to communicate in ways that we don't understand. All the molecules seem to know what the others are doing and then behave in synchronization. The system reorganizes out of chaos at the critical point of instability. Again, perhaps individual particles or objects are really not separate; perhaps they are interconnected—both separate and unified—a duality of nature. In the words of Ilya Prigogine, "[Chemical clocks] show that the reacting mixture is not chaotic, but there is actually a coherence. There is the possibility of chemical communication between molecules over long distances" (cited in Tucker, 1983, p. 88). In terms of real-world application, organizational change consultant Price Pritchett (1994) implored, "A rapidly changing world deals ruthlessly with organizations that don't change. . . . Perpetual change will be crucial if the organization is to survive in the years to come" (p. 14).

Fields, Forces, Fractals, and Other Funny Things

Morphogenic fields are another example of phenomenon that strain the Western brain. Species' collective memories, such as the cases of a squirrel not being worried at the site of a rabbit but running away at the site of a cat (both rabbit and cat seen for the first time), and each proceeding generation of people being able to learn how to ride a bike quicker than previous generations, are wonderful examples of morphogenic fields.

We learn from morphogenic fields that there is a subliminal or other type of interconnectedness in people and nature that we cannot see. We should be more open to looking for these connections and relationships, and we should seek not to control, but to let them flow naturally.

Fractals prove to be yet another mysterious phenomenon in nature that can teach us important lessons. Examples of fractals can be seen in everyday life; they can be created in the laboratory; and, they can be created with a computer. Fractals are images that continually repeat themselves in finer and finer detail within a particular object. In nature, we see fractals in ferns, in mountains, in trees, and in clouds. Likewise, the human nervous system, circulatory system, and respiratory system are all examples of fractals, too. We learn a very special message from fractals. We learn that by trying to measure or observe something in ever increasing detail only moves us further from the full picture of reality. Rather, we must look outward to the macroscopic picture. From fractals we learn to look for patterns and recurring themes over the entire system; we must be patient.

People working within systems can also learn valuable lessons from slime mold, of all things. (This is not a reference to their bosses.) Slime mold is another example of duality in nature. In this case, thousands of single cell creatures live separate lives eating rotting logs on the forest floor. When their food source becomes extinct, they miraculously come together as a new, single creature. This creature then moves like a snail to a new food source. The new organism then becomes a plantlike fungus. It then erupts into thousands of new spores and starts a new cycle all over again. While the message is beginning to sound repetitive in this book, again we learn that far-reaching communication across a system is central to an organism's survival. Even further, we learn that apparently separate things are somehow interconnected, and systems may have broader definitions than we sometimes are led to believe.

LESSONS

Quantum physics and the other new sciences have taught us some valuable lessons. Some of these lessons seem like common sense, and so they support some of the existing work of various people and organizations. Other lessons are counterintuitive, and they make us strain to understand their meanings and applications. Some of these require a great "leap of faith" while others feel more natural. In any case, a summary of these key lessons follows below (Rettig, 2001):

(1) *With a duality in nature, there is also complementarity and uncertainty.* People have the natural tendency to make life easier to understand, so we categorize things and identify things and people as black and white. This either/or labeling is too simple and ultimately blinds us from truly understanding the truth. While

there are clearly dual identities in nature, they are cooperative not competitive, by and large. For example, the brain has two hemispheres that do have some specific functions. The left brain is understood to be linear and rational, while the right brain is holistic and intuitive. However, looking at the brain as two separate halves is surely a mistake. They work in concert together to be one brain. They complement one another (Waldrop, 1992). When we create a duality without the complementarity in our understanding of organizations and their people, we limit ourselves from seeing the full picture, and we subsequently attempt to solve problems with simplistic solutions.

(2) *People and systems are subjective and cannot be observed objectively.* Objectivity is an illusion, and measurement is subsequently subjective. How we see the world is less a matter of reality than a matter of what we choose to see. However, we help to create reality by our participation. Observation is a form of participation. We cannot be separate from what we observe. University of Oregon physicist Amit Goswami stated, "Quantum mechanics is fraught with certain paradoxes, but these are paradoxes only when we look at them from the point of view of scientific realism—that reality exists independent of us, the observers" (1996, p. 51).

From Bell's Theorem we learn that the effects that our measurements are designed to measure may well not draw a direct line back to a particular cause. Jungian analyst Victor Mansfield and physicist Marvin Spiegelman (1996) reasoned:

We must now abandon our servitude to strict causality, the idea that all events have some well-defined set of causes and that the same initial conditions always generate the same effects. Now we must learn to appreciate that although nature is structured and lawful, it is acausal. (p. 192)

And, as nature is inherently subjective, our intuitions are reasonable insights to accept and even to encourage in our employees. Since natural phenomena are subjective by nature, rather than objective, prediction and replication are inherently futile and impossible to do effectively.

(3) *All of nature is unified and interconnected.* We are part of nature and are thus interconnected with all of nature and each other.

"The implications of this are profound. . . . the physical world is an inseparable whole" (Gilman, 1993, p. 12). This concept supports the point that we are part of what we observe, not separate from it. How can we be interconnected with what we are observing, yet not influence it? "We have finally come to see the world as a single, albeit complicated, system, one immense set of interrelated pieces" (Lipman-Blumen, 1996, p. 78). Communication is critical to the unification of the system/organization. In terms of school systems, Patrick Dolan (1994, p. 63) stated, "The first issue of systems-thinking is that the critical phenomena are *not* [emphasis in original] the individual parts, but how they fit together. This is a network of relationships deeply interconnected. Each one of the 'sub-systems' is somehow defined by its position to the others." Furthermore, instantaneous communication at a distance may be the glue to this unification.

(4) *A web of relationships is central to this unification.* Just as living systems are integrated wholes, so too is everyone and everything interconnected. Therefore, identifying and embracing the web of relationships internal and external to the system is imperative. Everyone receives their identity from each other, and in turn, create the identity of everyone else. "Managerial work today is less about wielding power than about coping with dependence . . . managers are put into a far more complex web of interaction with influential others than any organization chart can suggest," according to Harvard University professor of business Dr. J. Kotter (1999, p. 4). Furthermore, measuring by taking apart the whole to observe individual parts takes one further away from reality. The whole can only be understood by looking at the whole as a system; it needs to be observed over the breadth of time and space. Once again, the whole is greater than the sum of its parts.

(5) *Changes at the local level can make huge impacts at the system level.* Education systems thinker Patrick Dolan (1994, p. xii) wrote, "The entire system is *one* [emphasis in original], and to change a school is to change a district, its union, board, and management." Margaret Wheatley (1994a) said it best:

"Think globally, act locally" expresses a quantum perception of reality. Acting locally is a sound strategy for changing the large system. . . . Acting locally allows us to work with the movement and flow of simultaneous

events within the small system. We are more likely to become synchro-
nized with that system, and thus to have an impact. These changes in small
places, however, create large-system changes . . . because they share in the
unbroken wholeness that has united them all along. Our activities in one
part of the whole create non-local causes that emerge far from us. (p. 42)

The butterfly effect gives inspiration to every member of the organization. It lends credibility to the leader in all of us.

(6) *What might appear to be chaos, may not actually be chaos, but may
    be an underlying order.* We need to take a look at the system as a
    unified whole over time and across the entire system. Furthermore,
    systems can survive only if they do change. We may not feel com-
    fortable with this lack of control, but it's a control that we really
    never had in the first place. We should embrace these fluctuations
    and changes as they are the process in which order becomes re-
    stored. Very often, change comes from disorder or chaos. The crit-
    ical point where a system can either jump to a higher level of or-
    ganization or fall into true disarray and die is called the bifurcation
    point. "Chaotic systems show the ability to destructure an old order
    in the presence of new conditions and subsequently to bifurcate
    into a new structure or order" (Goswami, 1996, p. 58). Sometimes,
    the system has to completely fall apart in order to reorganize. We
    hurt the system by trying to control it and maintain equilibrium. In
    other words, we must let the system—or encourage it to—naturally
    move into disorder. In order to make an organization best able to
    survive in an ever-changing environment, "The workforce should
    always be empowered to run in new directions" (Kotter, 1999, p.
    20). And, control is an illusion and "leads to boundary building,
    turf protection, and assigning individual responsibility for results"
    (Gelatt, 1995, p. 111). So, workers must become comfortable with
    uncertainty and rely on their intuition. In addition, perhaps homo-
    geneity is analogous to equilibrium. Perhaps diversity and diversi-
    fication is a natural way for a system to evolve and to survive.

Ronald Pine (2000) wrote a truly awesome message that serves as an
inspiring conclusion to this chapter:

Quantum theory pictures the particles that make up everything that we
touch and feel not as little, hard, definite, independent things, but as a

tangle of possibilities entangled with every other tangle of possibilities throughout the universe. As with the particles in the Aspect experiment, the particles of my body may be connected in some way with the particles of your body, and these in turn with particles in a distant sun, in a distant galaxy, billions of light-years away. (p. 237)

POINTS TO PONDER

1. What lessons from these new sciences is Leslie incorporating into her work life?
2. Where is Leslie's thinking mired in traditional organizational thinking?
3. How could Leslie change this? What should she do differently?
4. Describe implications for leadership, as learned from the quantum physics.
5. Describe implications for leadership, as learned from the other new sciences.
6. What are some other implications you have found that are not covered in this chapter?

CHAPTER 6

Conclusions for Educational Leadership Practice

[This] creative process is much like Shiva's dance in Indian mythology. Shiva, Nataraja, the king of the dancers, dances under a halo of cosmic flame. In one hand, he holds fire to destroy the known world, to bring chaos and to destructure the old order; in the other hand, he holds a drum with which to welcome the new creation, the new order. In this integrated description of creation dynamics, the crucial features of the underlying mechanism are chaotic destructuring, unconscious proliferation of coherent superpositions, quantum leaps of insight, and chaotic restructuring.

—Goswami, 1996, p. 59

LESLIE'S LAMENT

As the conference group came back to the circle, Leslie glanced out the window and noticed that the rain had stopped and the sun had come out. Marva had a gentle smile on her face. She started with a quote from Albert Einstein, "No problem can be solved from the same consciousness that created it. We must learn to see the world anew."

"I want to reiterate what Woodrow said as he concluded before break. The sciences that you learned in school were good. It is their continued application to areas outside of science that is wrong. We need a new way of thinking about our organizations. We need to apply the lessons from these newer sciences. And to be honest, these newer sciences aren't that new. Scientists have been working on them for at least half a century. It's just the general public hasn't been listening. We're comfortable with our misapplications."

Marva continued, "But, let's move forward." She began with some background on quantum physics, yet she made certain to not bring any mathematics into the dialogue. She then split the large group into six smaller groups. Each subgroup was given a couple of articles and summaries to read. Two of the groups were given articles and summaries on the topic of the double slit experiment, two other groups on Schrodinger's Cat, and two groups on Bell's Theorem. "I want you to read the articles and summaries for your group. Then, answer the following questions:

1) What is the science? In other words, what is your topic about, scientifically?
2) Give examples, or describe it.
3) What lessons can we take from it?
4) How can we apply it to our workplace?"

The groups had one hour to get their tasks accomplished. They came back an hour later to make mini-presentations to their compatriots. Marva helped them along when they struggled. After each group made its presentation, the larger group was encouraged to digest and dialogue about questions 3 and 4. This took them right up to lunch.

Lunch was a tasty buffet served by the chef of the Vista Resort. It was a great assortment of warm and cold foods. Suffice it to say, everyone was satisfied. While not required, people in the group were encouraged to sit with people they didn't know or with whom they didn't work very closely. Leslie didn't like this idea, yet she knew its importance. Leslie sat across the table from Maxine, the wife of CEO Bernard. To Leslie's left sat Momar, the budget director at Cindy's work. To her right sat Don, a sales executive colleague of Cindy and Momar. People could talk about what they learned at the morning's session, or they could talk about any other topic.

As was to be expected, Leslie's group spent much of the first part of lunch talking about what their jobs entailed and about family things. Maxine was a recently retired school teacher. She had taught high school social studies in Santa Fe, New Mexico. Collecting Native American artwork and crafts was her hobby. She had two grown children—twins. One was a musician in a jazz band and the other was a CPA. "How that ever happened, God only knows!" exclaimed Maxine. Momar had lived in the United States for the past seven years. He grew up in Eastern Africa. He attended college in the States. Momar lived alone, but loved to listen to music from all around the world. Poetry was his passion. Don was also single, but had just started dating a young woman who was a graduate school student in the college of communications at the university. Don grew up in San Francisco and loved to travel. He didn't like to spend too long in any one place. He had lived in Britton for six months, and this new job was perfect for his wandering appetite.

After lunch, the group got back together. Marva followed the same format, but this time the six groups received articles and summaries on chaos theory, dissipative structures and chemical clocks, and on fields, forces, and fractals. They had one more hour to complete their new tasks and one hour to present and dialogue in the larger group.

Surprisingly, the group seemed to enjoy the tasks. Good dialogue came out of it and the time moved swiftly. Since the day had warmed up nicely, into the upper 50s, and everything was dry outside, Marva asked everyone to do an assignment outside. "We have one-half hour before our day is done. I would like to request each of you to take your note pads outside. Find a comfortable place to sit, or stand, I don't care. Walk around if you'd prefer. Anyway, make a journal entry. Write anything that strikes you. I would suggest only that you focus your attention to what you learned today—to something that has lit a fire in you, and something that you want to learn more about. We'll share those, if you wish, tomorrow morning before we jump in with our agenda. How does that sound?"

Everyone walked outside. Most people sat down quickly once they found their little place of solitude. Leslie and a handful of others decided to walk around the woods and the pond. "I'll journal when I get home tonight. I'm just going to enjoy this beauty right now," Leslie mused to herself.

Leslie's head was swimming when she got home. After eating a chef salad, Leslie sat down on her futon with a glass of Merlot and her journal. She wrote,

> Today was really fun and exhausting. It has been so good to meet new people. I need to get out more often. I seemed to learn so much about these new sciences, but I don't really seem to know anything. I'm so tired, but so wide awake. I want to learn a lot on chaos theory. I've got to get James Gleick's book *Chaos: Making a New Science*. Tomorrow has me intrigued. I really want to get down to the application. Will this stuff really be applicable to our lives? No more thinking tonight. Good night.

THE SCIENCE

Now that the lessons from quantum physics and the other new sciences have been identified, let's return our focus to application of the lessons to several key areas of schools' systems. As was mentioned in the beginning of this book, school organization and communication, teacher supervision and evaluation, curriculum/instruction and student assessment, and budgeting are but a few critical elements in education that are affected by our scientific stances.

ORGANIZATIONAL STRUCTURE AND COMMUNICATION

If indeed we believe that human organizations (e.g., school systems) are dynamic, living organizations, then the impact of these new sciences on education could be profound. "Living systems macroscopically appear as open, dissipative, far from equilibrium systems, equipped with many macroscopic configurations (complex system)" (Vitiello, 1995, p. 382). School systems should have less internal isolation with silos and departments and should be more integrated horizontally and vertically. As information is the lifeblood of living organizations, communication from the top to the bottom and across the organization must be able to move quickly throughout the entire system, and information should not be left in the hands of the few. Moreover, leaders of these systems must become more comfortable with ambiguity and with long-term goals, and be less concerned with control. In the words of Margaret Wheatley (1994b, p. 20), "Leaders need to stop managing moments and analyzing results day by day, or even quarter by quarter, and look for deeper order that shows up as patterns of behavior." Fritjof Capra (1996) explained the new structure:

> There is another kind of power, one that is more appropriate for the new paradigm—power as influence of others. The ideal structure for exerting this kind of power is not the hierarchy but the network. . . . The paradigm shift thus includes a shift in social organization from hierarchies to networks. (p. 10)

Similarly, these organizational structures must be fluid and flexible. People must not be organized in rigid permanent structures. Rather, they must be able to divide and join other people immediately for evolving tasks and then divide again just as quickly. Just like slime molds, the various people must come together and recreate, then depart again. In organizations, new leaders can emerge for a particular task, and then after the project is completed, go back to their usual tasks. In other words, people within organizations (and even external to the organizations) must be able to quickly respond to changing conditions and reorganize for the new task at hand. Each time, different leaders may emerge to meet these tasks. Lipman-Blumen (1996) posited:

> Unlike the rigid hierarchies of formal organizations, the informal system may be composed of many loosely structured webs, outside the chain of reporting channels. More flexible than hierarchies, network segments can operate separately. They even break away temporarily for specific purposes and the regroup without damage—sometimes in new configurations. (p. 210)

Thus, the new school system needs to be less concerned with command and control. It must focus less on maintaining its present structure of departments and bureaucratic functions, and focus more on networking together all the people within the system. Charles Handy—former professor at the London Business School—wrote, "In the future, we can see that organizations will be very different, much more like networks than machines" (1996, p. 3). More time should be spent on focusing on serving the clients—the teachers and students in the classrooms—and less on serving the dictates of administration. At times the system may need a major change in order to survive. It is then the leader's role to cause this to happen. Patrick Dolan (1994, p. 57) suggested, "The way you move a Steady State is to 'torque' the roles and relationships to create such unbearable tension at one place or another that the entire system suddenly slips, realigns, and finds itself in a different place." Chairman of Service Master C. William Pollard (1996, p. 245) concurred, "Leaders make things happen. They are responsible for initiating and, in some cases, creating disequilibrium in order to maintain the vitality of the organization they lead." These organizational experts are asking leaders to move their organizations to the bifurcation point. Furthermore, they must look at the whole picture over time and space, but they can focus their efforts at the site-level. Think globally, act locally. Managers are hired to maintain the status quo. Leaders are hired to make change. This is the Principle of Complementarity at its best. Both managers and leaders are needed and must work together.

Schedules and schedule integration may need to see changes, as well (Bransford, Brown, & Cocking, 1999, p. 140). Education expert Linda Darling-Hammond surmised, "To improve student learning, schools will need structures and schedules that provide time for complex teaching and long-term relationships, conditions that give serious, ongoing assistance to learners" (1999, p. 32).

School systems administrators are always looking for model programs that they can replicate throughout the system. They are looking for the best parent involvement program, the best reading model, the best approach to keep kids off of drugs. The list of model programs is indeed endless. However, the search for program replication is in vain. Nature, and therefore our social systems, are not linear. "[Nature] is acausal—the same initial conditions do not always generate the same effects" (Mansfield & Spiegelman, 1996, p. 192). Leaders need to stop looking to replicate programs and to be less concerned with apparent chaos. After all, order comes from chaos. Each system needs to examine its own unique identity and context, and then create programs for its own special features. Replication will not work, but it may still be entirely appropriate to look at other programs and see how they can be redesigned for a school's particular unique needs and characteristics.

SUPERVISION AND EVALUATION OF STAFF

As administration becomes less concerned with controlling and managing, their focus for teacher supervision and evaluation must change accordingly. Since living organizations are so highly complex and interconnected, it is impossible to draw a line of cause and effect—tug on one strand of the web and the whole web trembles. Therefore, it is imperative that administration abandon the reductionist philosophy of checklists to measure teacher skill parts. Rather, supervisors should spend a great deal of time looking for patterns and emerging themes. This will require long looks over space and time. To put it differently, supervisors need to examine the effectiveness of the entire system working together year after year, not on singular lessons from one teacher at a time. Furthermore, supervisors should welcome their intuitions. In the words of George B. Weber, secretary-general of the International Federation of Red Cross and Red Crescent Societies, "Intuition and the ability to deal with nonverbal signs of communication will also be critical skills for the leader of the future" (1996, p. 308). They should run away from the felt need to control through the objective lens and embrace the subjective nature of working with people.

Since every teacher and every classroom situation is unique, a one-size-fits-all approach to supervising teachers is clearly inappropriate. With that said, a differentiated supervision model like that espoused by Glickman, Gordon, and Ross-Gordon (1998) would be most beneficial. In this model the supervisor works with each unique teacher in a very unique way. Some teachers in some situations will need a great deal of direction through the "directive approach," while other teachers in other situations would initiate a "nondirective" approach from the supervisor. Different teachers in different situations could fall in anywhere in between this continuum including "directive informational" and "collaborative." This model can be used for working with individual teachers or groups of teachers, alike. This is a model that is more natural in that it is not a one-size-fits-all approach to supervision and to working with groups. Perhaps just as importantly, it starts with the premise that most teachers are professional and caring individuals who are self-directed.

Finally, since we know that different leaders emerge in order to respond to the changing environment, the entire supervisory process can now be shared by all the professionals within the system. In terms of professional development, different teachers and administrators have different strengths. Thus, when a particular strength is needed (e.g., knowledge of a certain subject or instructional strategy), a particular teacher may step forward to share leadership in the supervisory process. Once the task at hand is completed, the teacher's role goes back to its previous status, or perhaps onward.

This is perhaps the most important lesson to learn—the leader's role with change. No longer will the role of the administrator be to control and evaluate. The role will now change to helping the professionals to build networks and to rely on one another. "The job becomes one of looking for opportunities to form teams, to augment communication around similar efforts in three of four classrooms, and also to look for similarities that begin to occur across the system" (Dolan, 1994, p. 93). Teachers need to become a part of their colleagues' networks. More time should be spent observing one another for the purpose of professional development, not for the purpose of accountability. Rather than becoming more and more isolated, teachers must search for relationship building. While moving from our current paradigm to this new way of thinking may feel chaotic, building-level leaders should feel comfortable. They should, in fact, move the system to its bifurcation point.

CURRICULUM AND INSTRUCTION AND ASSESSMENT

As teachers expand their networks, they will take on more active roles in curriculum and instruction. Fewer levels of bureaucracy will permit information to flow quicker and the information will be more appropriately used by those working most closely with the customers. Rather than standardizing curriculum, materials, and pedagogy, individual teachers and school sites must be given the opportunity to react to the particular needs of their unique students. To put it differently, as organizations are fluid and ever changing, so too are people. Thus, teachers must be able to respond to their own classes with unique approaches. Standardization can only guarantee mediocrity. Standardization is a clear example of a system at equilibrium. This act of control only serves to stifle creativity and system growth. It means eventual death of the system.

The curriculum and pedagogy themselves will also need to change if we take the lessons of quantum physics and the other new sciences to heart. As was mentioned earlier in this book, the science of behaviorism became the model of teaching at the same time that traditional or classical organizational models came into existence. Behaviorism is a model or philosophy of education that is teacher-directed and work-sheet-driven. Students are expected to work independently and to memorize or accomplish a more and more difficult series of skill units. On the other hand, "Constructivism is open-ended, as is the neural structure of the brain" (Abbott & Ryan, 1999, p. 71). Citing the work of Feldman (1994) and then Wilson and Daviss (1994), Abbott and Ryan (1999) added,

> As scientists study learning, they are realizing that a constructivist model reflects their best understanding of the brain's natural way of making sense of the world. . . . A person learning something new brings to that experience . . . previous knowledge of the world into a unique pattern, connecting each new fact, experience, or understanding . . . into rational and meaningful relationships to the wider world. (p. 67)

The quantum world would seem to support the educational philosophy of constructivism where depth versus breadth of curriculum is the focus. It is much more student-centered with a great emphasis on social learning that is problem-based. Patterns and themes emerge as students work on the whole topic, rather than focus on isolated parts or isolated skills. Cross-curricular planning is most appropriate, and the entire curriculum is sufficiently flexible to meet the needs of the children. In other words, curriculum planning starts with the focus on the children, not on the content. Bransford and his associates (1999) stipulated:

> It is the network, the connection among objectives, that is important. . . . Stress on isolated parts can train students in a series of routines without educating them to understand an overall picture that will ensure the development of integrated knowledge structures and information about conditions of applicability. An alternative to simply progressing through a series of exercises that derive from a scope and sequence chart is to expose students to the major features of a subject domain as they arise naturally in problem situations. Activities can be structured so that students are able to explore, explain, extend, and evaluate their progress. (p. 127)

Since many educators are looking to see how the brain works, it might be helpful to note that some researchers are convinced that quantum physics is the appropriate science to study the brain (Amoroso & Martin, 1995; Gould, 1995; Vitiello, 1995; and Walker, 2000). In his book that pushes the envelope of the application of quantum physics, *The Dreaming Universe,* Fred Alan Wolf postulated, "The dream state is representative of superpositions of brain-generated quantum waves or quantum states. . . . Thus it is necessary to look at neural networks using quantum states rather than Boolean binary states" (1994, p. 165). Schwartz and Russek (1999, p. 157) wrote, "Children should be taught to think systemically from a very early age. There may be critical periods when the human mind and brain may be especially open to learning how to think and feel systemically." Other areas of our school services and curriculum might see changes. From guidance counseling to the arts and to the psychology of learning, modifications could be made. Mansfield and Spiegelman (1996) have posited that the relationship between therapist and patient works at a quantum level. Certainly teachers and guidance counselors would find direct parallels in their daily work. Even more, Goswami (1996) proposed that creativity in children comes for those "who experience a personal sense of purpose in tune with the purpose of the universe" (p. 55). Finally, perhaps the study of quantum physics and the other newer sciences should be integrated into the curriculum—a curriculum where intuition is encouraged. "Physics curricula of the twenty-first century could include classes in meditation" (Zukav, 1980, p. 310). Furthermore, at least introductory units in quantum physics and these other newer sciences should be taught in our schools. If students only learn the classical sciences, we may never be able to see life through a different lens—we may be doomed to repeat the errors of our past. "If you always do what you've always done, you will always get what you always got." All these curricular and pedagogical ideas might often appear to be chaotic; well, so too is real life.

Likewise, assessment of student learning must change if we have learned our lessons from these sciences. Since constructivism provides for more authentic learning than behaviorism, it would follow that student assessment should also be more authentic. Teachers, and the students themselves, should use a variety of sources to help them determine the extent of student learning. However, as always when making measurements in this quantum world, we would be well advised to heed the words of Patrick Dolan (1994, p. 21), "The numbers may be true, but they are not the truth." Since everything is networked together, we should focus our observations holistically, not on the measurement of tiny skill parts. We should also look for understanding over time, not discrete moments.

But on the other side of the coin, Margaret Wheatley (1994a, p. 63) warned us, "Every act of measurement loses more information than it obtains." Measurement of humans is inherently subjective. Again, the observer or measurer cannot separate herself or himself from the measurement. The very act of observation influences the measurement as all the potential "vector states" collapse into one. In *Quantum Reality: Beyond the New Physics,* Nick Herbert implored, "If we take quantum theory seriously as a picture of what's really going on, each measurement does more than disturb it: it profoundly reshapes the very fabric of reality" (cited in Pine, 2000, p. 222). Indeed, by observing, we are helping to create reality. From quantum physics we have learned that every potential outcome is merely a probability. We can never know for certain the extent of our accuracy. So, all measurements should be taken with a very strong grain of salt.

BUDGETING

Even the apparently clear-cut, linear function of school system budgeting can take cues from quantum physics and the other newer sciences.

While traditional methods of accounting systems and accountability must not change, the focus of dispersing school funding should probably see some changes. As quantum physics seems to support site-based decision making, so too, these new sciences seem to support more local site control of the system budget. As singular school sites must be able to adapt quickly to the changing environment and needs, more financial resources will be needed at the individual schools to support their work. Perhaps less rigid mandates from federal and state agencies may be needed. These rigid mandates demand replication and standardization and often do not allow for creative solutions and quick responses.

In order to survive in these quickly changing times, and in order to be most effective and efficient in so doing, individual school sites should have access to a much larger portion of the system's budget. For example, more and more school districts are allowing individual sites to control such functions of the budget as salaries (through deciding how and whom to hire), technology purchases, and even capital improvements. These schools are able to move larger portions of the budget around quickly to meet current challenges. Likewise, more and more schools are using a modified approach to zero-based budgeting. In this way, each teacher and/or department must annually redefine their individual allocations for budgets. Long gone are the times where each teacher or department is guaranteed a routine line item amount in the budget. Changing needs require changing budgetary demands. And finally, as we will recall, while site-based budgeting and decision making may appear to be chaotic and out of control, there quite likely is an overarching order in it all. At the very least individual sites will better be able to respond to their particular environments and needs.

THE QUANTUM SCHOOL

There are more schools perhaps than we know that are already using many of these quantum principles. As has been mentioned numerous times in this book, quantum physics is an intuitive science, and good school leaders are abandoning linear approaches to administration and following their intuitive instincts. What characteristics would you find in quantum schools?

Loosely coupled schools, as purported by Bolman and Deal, just may be the epitome of a natural, living organization. These schools are fluid, and they are forever structuring and restructuring. Quantum schools and school systems are structured to allow decision making at the most basic level. These schools are more site-based in governance and allow for much more teacher autonomy. Work groups of teachers (and at the classroom level—students) quickly move in and out of teams in order to most effectively meet the task at hand. Budgets are fluid and flexible and support building-level and teacher autonomy.

The curriculum and pedagogy are necessarily constructivist-based, which allows for student-centered instruction and social learning. The content is more problem-based around themes and is cross-curricular in nature. In all likelihood, classrooms are less grade-based and provide for looping or block scheduling. As information is the life-blood of any living organization, a vast array of measurements are used to determine student learning. But the focus is on improvement of instruction and helping students grow, rather than merely on accountability. In the words of Noam Chomsky (2000):

> A good teacher knows that the best way to help students learn is to allow them to find the truth by themselves. Students don't learn by a mere transfer of knowledge, consumed through rote memorization and later regurgitated. True learning comes about through the discovery of truth, not through the imposition of an official truth. (p. 21)

Administrators' roles are different in a quantum school. They are in an opportune position to see the whole picture, over space and time. Their job is to support those closest to the classroom, to make connections and build relationships among the various staff. They continually search for ways to provide the lifeblood, information, to all members of the system. Because, metaphorically speaking, people are like atoms that are looking for relationships to happen (Wheatley, 1994b), leaders encourage and develop the talents of everyone to be leaders and then make leadership connections as needed. They spend much less time observing, supervising, and evaluating teachers for accountability purposes, and spend much more time connecting the teachers together for both professional development and in order to meet the students' unique needs. In other words, administrators make a quantum leap from management to true leadership. Organizational leaders and theorists know these lessons well. From Rosabeth Moss Kanter (1996) professor of the Harvard Business School, to James Heskett and Leonard Schlessinger (1996)—professors of the Harvard Graduate School of Business and the

Harvard Business School, respectively—to Dave Ulrich (1996)—professor of the School of Business at the University of Michigan—and to Marshall Goldsmith (1996)—business consultant—we learn of the need for organizational leaders to take an active role in relationship building. These leadership gurus and authors have teamed together to share a new vision. In the words of F. Hesselbein, president of the Peter F. Drucker Foundation for Nonprofits Management, "The new design [takes] people out of the boxes of the old hierarchy and move[s] them into a more circular, flexible, and fluid management system that spell[s] liberation of human spirit and endeavor" (1996, p. 122).

In sum, these new sciences have taught us that everything is interconnected and that creating relationships and networks is a central task of school leaders. Our organizations should be structured in such a way that encourages these connections to come and go as appropriate. "If we are willing to think outside the box created by Frederick Taylor and his colleagues so many decades ago, we can imagine and create schools that provide real time and focus for both student and teacher learning" (Darling-Hammond, 1999, p. 36). Teacher supervision and evaluation should also focus on relationship-building. The question should always be asked, "How is the whole system working together to meet the needs of the children?" The curriculum and instruction should focus on the children and encourage holistic and authentic learning with an emphasis on themes and patterns. Assessment of student learning should be done across space and time. In other words, many different types of measurement over time should be used. Multiple methods of longitudinal measurements for each student would be appropriate. Hopefully qualitative research is viewed at least, if not more, as credibly as quantitative research. According to quantum physics and the other newer sciences, much of what we already believe intuitively is sound educational practice. By making slight modifications in our system structures, our human connections, and in some of our curricular focus, we can make a huge impact on education. These lessons are all too important. Educational leadership prophet John Gardiner warned us, "The future of our planet and its life forms depends on increasing the level of authentic relationship among human beings" (1998, p. 118). Think globally, act locally. But we do know that we will be challenged every step of the way. In the words of Jean Lipman-Blumen (1996, p. 94), "Certainly, the connective leaders who do emerge can expect to meet resistance from old-style leaders and their followers, who remain locked behind the mental bars of individualistic, competitive leadership paradigms."

But . . .
Here I stand; I can do no other.
(Martin Luther)

POINTS TO PONDER

1. How is Leslie beginning to change her perceptions of working within school organizations?
2. What do you think Leslie now feels about supervision and evaluation of teachers?
3. How should school systems change their organizational structure and improve communication?
4. How should teacher supervision and evaluation be changed?
5. How should curriculum, instruction, and assessment be changed?
6. How should the school budget process be improved?
7. Write your own description of the "quantum school."

Epilogue

We shall not cease from exploration
And the end of all our exploring
Will be to arrive where we started
And know the place for the first time

—T. S. Eliot (cited in Jaworski, 1996, p. 187)

LESLIE'S LAMENT

Marva began Friday morning off by playing a smooth jazz CD as background music. Everyone was standing around pouring coffee or juice and nibbling on a wide assortment of bagels with cream cheese and jams. Marva dimmed the lights and then brought them back up halfway, and the group came back together at their seats in the circle. Several sticks of sandstone incense were burning throughout the room. "Would anyone like to share their journals?"

Bernard waited to see if anyone wanted to share first, but since no one leaped in, he started, "I've been to this workshop before, and that's why I have brought Marva and Woodrow here to be with us. While the science thrills me, I am more energized by the impact I see on the organization. For the first time, I can see people constantly challenging the way things are done. They are looking outside their own little departments. They are looking at their customers first. But, I don't want to say any more at this time. I want the dialogue to come from everyone here."

Leslie was surprised to see Cindy enter the dialogue. "Now I'm sure I'm as confused as everyone else here, but that's all right. I can live with some uncertainty. Isn't that just the point? Uncertainty. We have to learn to live in a world of uncertainty. We have been taught the fallacy that we can be objective and predict the future in our organizations. These new sciences seem to be telling us that that is impossible. We automatically influence whatever we're trying to observe and analyze, and then prediction is fruitless. Is that correct?"

Marva had a friendly smile on her face. "That is such a super question, Cindy. And I can't answer that with a yes/no response. We have been taught about objectivity and prediction in regard to closed, mechanical systems. For those kinds of systems, indeed we can be more objective and predict what will happen. We can predict that putting sand in your gas tank will ruin your engine. We can objectively observe this. We can do these things because your car is a closed machine. On the other hand, open and dynamic systems are really impossible to observe objectively and to make accurate predictions. Does that make sense?"

"I can live with that," Cindy responded.

Not to be outdone by her sister, Leslie announced, "I love science. Why is it that we haven't learned about these new sciences when we were kids?" Leslie gulped as she knew the answer.

Marva questioned Leslie, "Well, do your schools teach them, today? The science has been there, but educators haven't kept up." Leslie sensed twenty-seven pairs of eyes looking at her.

Leslie's new friend, Maxine, came to the rescue. "Marva, it seems to me that these new sciences are telling us that the old hierarchies and two-way communication patterns are ineffective and inefficient. Can you give us examples?"

"Maxine, you're correct. We are learning that human organizations must become much more elaborately structured. They must allow for new groups of people to be able to come together quickly in order to respond to issues or to plan, and then to be able to dissolve just as quickly. These systems must be very fluid. Hence the need for complex networking and relationships. Everyone within the organization must be connected to one another. As far as examples, we'll get to that later."

Maxine nodded and Marva moved on. "I think it's best to summarize the lessons we have learned." On a flip-chart, Marva listed:

Quantum Physics and the other new sciences tell us

- with a duality in nature, there is also complementarity and uncertainty

- people and systems are subjective and cannot be observed objectively
- all of nature is unified and interconnected
- a web of relationships is central to this unification
- change at the local level can make huge impacts at the system level
- what might appear to be chaos may not actually be chaos, but may actually be an underlying order

After Marva led the group in a dialogue about these key points, Woodrow stood up. "Now it's time to start getting down to application. Maxine, perhaps we will cover examples here. Let's take a look at one particular area of our organizations—how they are structured. Let's begin by describing how they look now. These will probably be described in terms of what I like to call, 'Newtonian Organizations.' We will then take a look at how they might be reorganized using the lessons we learned from these new sciences."

Woodrow asked the group to begin brainstorming out loud different descriptors for their organizational structures. A chaotic barrage followed: "top-down, boring, standardization, control, prediction, specialization, bureaucracy, isolation, flow-charts, objectivity."

"Whoa, I think we've got a plethora of characteristics of the old organizations. Now . . ."

Hurriedly, Mike Magnum interjected, "Woodrow, I'm sorry for interrupting, but I have to mention something that has been concerning me. I like to know what is expected of me. I like to know from day-to-day what I will be doing. I like to be able to plan my target activities and then monitor my progress. Am I all wet?"

Woodrow paused. He didn't know how to explain to Mike that he was going to have to learn how to live without his security blanket. Finally he said, "Mike, I understand you. I think you're feeling fear of the unknown. Unfortunately, or maybe fortunately, in today's new systems approach, we have to be able to learn to live with change and the unknown. In fact, I think the only way to survive is to embrace chaos and change. The more we try to control," Woodrow clenched his fist out in front of him for affect, "the more we squeeze life out of the organization. We have to learn to let go and to go for a ride."

Mike wasn't happy, but what could he do? So, he nodded politely.

Woodrow knew it was best to move on. "Now let's take a look at this list and see if we have different descriptors for these new organizations.

What are some words that you would think we should use for these new organizations—using the lessons we learned from the newer sciences?"

Just as quickly as before, the words came spewing forth: "sharing, caring, networks, web of relationships, subjectivity, illusion, uncertainty, chaos, fun, evolution, multi-tasking, Neo-Renaissance-person."

The latter word brought a good laugh from everyone. Woodrow asked Bernard to explain. "My reasoning for this," Bernard began, "is because the Renaissance person was known for the ability to do so many things. He or she could handle a wide variety of responsibilities and was not isolated of too highly specialized. I think that is what is required from today's worker, but with many levels of technology and at a faster pace. If we are to be able to respond quickly to various issues, our workers will have to have the ability to do many different kinds of jobs and move within them with ease—the Neo-Renaissance person."

Bernard continued, "I know we have the capacity to be the Neo-Renaissance people and organizations, but we are only limited by our own fears. I think to varying degrees, we are already acting in this capacity, on individual bases. We have to reinvent our organizations to best support this capacity."

Woodrow nodded approvingly. He then put a transparency on the screen. "I took these notes from a video by Dr. Margaret Wheatley & CRM Films. The video is entitled, 'Leadership and the New Science,' which has come directly from her book with the same title. In fact, if you read any book because of these past two days, please get this one. You'll love it, and it is very readable. Anyway, let me get to this transparency."

SHIFTS IN SCIENTIFIC AND ORGANIZATIONAL THINKING
   Shift 1—From the parts to the whole
   Shift 2—From understanding processes rather than structures
   Shift 3—To understanding that the universe is a web of relationships, constantly shifting and growing
   Shift 4—Towards the realization that we can never know reality absolutely or predict anything
   Source: Wheatley, M. (1993). *Leadership and the new science.* Videorecording and Instructor's Manual. Carslbad, CA: CRM Films.

UNDER THE LENS OF NEW SCIENCE
   • Order found in chaos
   • Strange attractors
   • Patterns or fractals in nature
   • Chaos as a route to order

- Relationships at the heart of all reality
- Vision as an energy field

Source: Wheatley, M. (1993). *Leadership and the new science.* Video-recording and Instructor's Manual. Carlsbad, CA: CRM Films.

After explaining Wheatley's position on these new concepts, Woodrow moved forward. "We've started off with some broadly defined descriptors of these new organizations. Now we've got to get down to some more detail, to some clearer ideas of application. Before lunch we will get to the task of organizational structure in our new organizations. After lunch, we will focus on communication, on budgeting, and on measurement of goals and performance evaluations. That's a lot to ask of us, but we'll see what we can accomplish."

Cindy and Leslie squeezed hands and gave each other grins of anticipation. It's as if they both were saying, "Performance evaluations—just what we've been waiting for!" Or, something to that effect.

Woodrow was cautious. "This next part always worries me. We come from different organizations, each very unique and idiosyncratic. Even more, we just got finished saying that we can't replicate complex systems. Yet, we want to get some decent idea of how to describe the structure of these new organizations. We just have to be careful not to think of this as a recipe or guide to follow. Your organizations must create this on their own. With that said, let's continue."

Bernard stood up. "At this time, I'd like everyone from our firm to get together as one group. Our guests can form another group. Before we get up to move around, here is our task for the next hour. We are going to have time only to begin this new dialogue. Our task is to imagine we are designing this as a brand new organization. With keeping the lessons of these past two days in mind, how would we optimally structure our organization in order to be most effective for the future? How can we create the organization to best support and unleash the capacity of our collective individuality? I will facilitate our firm's group with a couple of activities. Woodrow and Marva will do the same for our guests' group. Let's begin!"

As they were waiting in the buffet line, Leslie and Cindy were all abuzz about the morning's activities and anticipation about those of the afternoon. Suddenly, Leslie felt a strange vibrating on her hip. Was she getting too worked up from all this? No, it was her pager. It must be truly urgent as Leslie told her secretary not to page unless there was an emergency. Leslie stepped out of line to call her office.

Leslie went back to join Cindy in line. "Cindy, I can't stay here this afternoon. My secretary called. She said that we've had a bomb threat. We've got to take this seriously, and I have to go. Please let me know how it goes!" Cindy gave Leslie a warm hug.

Cindy gave Leslie a call that night to tell her about the afternoon's activities. "Did you catch who called in the bomb threat?"

Leslie was clearly saddened. "Yes, and now—by board policy—we have to proceed with expulsion hearings. I don't know if I'm more disappointed in the child or in the fact that I thought our nice community school was beyond that. I mean, I thought we were such a good family. It's so disheartening."

Cindy decided to pick things up. "Well, hopefully I can help. Bernard told me of a two-credit course the university is offering. It's entitled, 'Leadership Takes a Quantum Leap.' Since you have to get credits to keep your license, we might as well do this together. It sounds like a blast. Two professors, one from the College of Business and one from the College of Education are teaching it. The class promises to be very similar to what we did these past two days. Its focus is on application for the practitioner. There is not supposed to be any math to worry about, but there will be many guest speakers. We get to read many of the books contained in the annotated bibliography that Marva and Woodrow gave to us, a lot of dialogue, and then some kind of community project."

Leslie was hooked. She and Cindy signed up via the Web.

Leslie and her ad hoc teacher supervision/evaluation committee met on Wednesday morning. Leslie was excited to hear the experiences the teachers had this past week. She was just as filled with anticipation about that night's class with Cindy.

As she was walking in Hannah proclaimed, "I must say that I'm pleasantly surprised. You know, I've had student teachers before, and this is kind of like that. But, I don't spend my time on monitoring, rather most of my time is spent listening. Mary wasn't intimidating about this at all."

Mary Thompson smiled. "I'm pleased to say that Hannah asked me to try this out. She asked me to come in to observe her teach the science unit on pollution that I created for the district. She wanted me to see if she was teaching it the way I had envisioned it. The observation could be meaningful for both of us that way. I think I got more out of it than she did."

Vicki quizzed Mary. "Well, how did it go? Did it go like you had envisioned?"

Mike Tippler also asked, "Did you have a preconference and post-conference like we do with Leslie?"

Mary continued by addressing Mike. "We did have a preconference in Hannah's classroom. The meeting only lasted about ten minutes. She told me why she wanted me to come in—to watch to see how effective my lesson design was and whether I would give her any hints about instruction. We talked casually about the students and about where they were in the unit. I went in to observe the next morning."

Hannah then took up the slack for Mary. "We postconferenced after school. I bet we spent at least half an hour. You know, I just thought of this—I didn't take any notes, but Mary did during our chat. I just listened and talked with her."

"That's right," Mary continued. "Hannah and I ultimately have the same philosophy about education, but sometimes we get to the end by different routes. So, while she didn't teach the lesson the way I had planned it, it really seemed to work for her. So, I took notes so that I could add a section to the unit planner that I created. I now have more ideas. That's why I think I benefited more from observing Hannah than she got from me. That really seems to be the crux of professional development."

Leslie nodded in agreement. "I know what you mean. I feel like I would be a better teacher now that I have observed so many good teachers. Mary, were you able to give Hannah any feedback?"

Mary hesitated. "You know, not really. I kept thinking about what I wanted to put into my unit planner. I guess I didn't focus the way I should have."

"I understand," Leslie said. "That is probably something that everyone would need to practice. Perhaps next time you could video tape Hannah, and then the two of you could sit down to view the tape together and learn from it."

"That sounds like a great idea!" Hannah exclaimed. Then the early bell rang.

Leslie concluded the meeting, "Would you all agree to share today's dialogue with the entire staff at next week's faculty meeting?" Everyone agreed.

THE FUTURE

While it would have been interesting to continue the story of Leslie's Lament or to follow her adventure in the other critical areas (besides teacher supervision and evaluation), it is not my intent to provide a recipe for the requisite changes needed in our school systems. As we have learned, each school and school system is so very unique. We cannot begin to replicate or predict how our own individual settings will be impacted. The readers must now begin their own stories.

As was mentioned much earlier, our system of public education is undoubtedly at a bifurcation point. The signs are here, but we may not even be noticing that we're at a bifurcation point. The public is demanding higher standards of teachers and of schools. They are experimenting with new types of schools with different foci in the curriculum. Our institution of public education may well be at the fulcrum of leaping to a higher order or simply dying away and being supplanted by something new. Our tendency is to tighten our control even harder, but this will only throw us back to equilibrium—a sure sign of death.

I don't know where this book will take us into the future. However, the intent of this book is to prime a new dialogue for educational leaders. Current models of educational leadership—more appropriately, administration—are mired in an approach that should never have been created. Its misapplication came from a science that is inappropriate for human and open, dynamic systems. This new line of observing and working within organizations is much more congruent with our actual experiences in these same human and open, dynamic systems. While I have not yet analyzed the conceptual parallels between the lessons of quantum physics and leadership approaches/models such as transformational leadership, value-added leadership, servant leadership, and of normative change processes, and spirituality, my intuition is that these are nearly a perfect match.

Furthermore, it is the intention of this book to serve as a catalyst for educational change. Therefore, while I covered the areas of organizational structure and communication; teacher supervision and evaluation; curriculum, instruction, and assessment; and budgeting, other areas could have been included. For example, other critical areas might have included scheduling, transportation, special education, collective bargaining, staff development, educational politics, policy development, federal and state roles, and so many others. Still, these four crucial areas should be sufficient for the reader to begin thinking anew. The reader is encouraged to share this book with her/his colleagues and begin an open dialogue with them. As networking and relationship-building is a central theme in this book, it would be most appropriate to expand this dialogue to individuals and groups throughout the community. After all, change such as this can most likely only occur with a grassroots effort.

Dr. Perry Rettig can be reached at rettig@uwosh.edu to continue this dialogue. The books and articles included in the annotated bibliography at the back of this book are meant to serve as primers to this new line of thinking about systems and educational leadership. They are all quite readable and should serve as catalysts for other readings and dialogue.

Annotated Bibliography

Block, P. (1996). *Stewardship: Choosing service over self-interest.* San Francisco: Berrett-Koehler. Peter Block's *Stewardship* is a must read for all persons with leadership responsibilities. Not only does Block call for an entirely unconventional relationship between administration and workers, he also explains how to get there. We are all responsible for one another—a truly interconnected web of life. This is a genuinely inspirational work of literature.

Capra, F. (1996). *The web of life: A new scientific understanding of living systems.* New York: Anchor Books Doubleday. This outstanding book weaves together a web of relationships of all the complex newer sciences. Less technical than most science books, it provides the reader with a quick yet satisfying understanding of all these new sciences. It will also provide the reader with strong insights into lessons we can learn from these sciences.

Csikszentmihalyi, M. (1990). *Flow: The psychology of optimal experience.* New York: HarperCollins. Mihaly Csikszentmihalyi has captured the essence of the new sciences without ever mentioning them. He brilliantly brings in personal and other people's life experiences that show the flow state. He paints a picture of how we can bring flow experiences into our personal and work lives. *Flow* captures the life of the new sciences.

Dolan, P. (1994). *Restructuring our schools: A primer on systemic change.* Kansas City, MO: Systems & Organizations. The designer of "The Village Partnership" begins this book with an intriguing study of the history of the classical model of leadership, and he explains why this model is inappropriate for our schools. The remaining two-thirds of this fast read details how school districts can actually restructure themselves while still operating under the old system.

Gardner, H. (1995). *Leading minds: An anatomy of leadership.* New York: Basic Books. Howard Gardner takes a look at ten contemporary leaders throughout the world. He devotes a chapter for each leader's biography.

From this framework, he draws out several underlying themes about what many of these great leaders have in common. This is a fascinating read for all students of leadership.

Hesselbein, F., Goldsmith, M., & Beckhard, R. (Eds.). (1996). *The leader of the future: The Drucker Foundation.* San Francisco: Jossey-Bass. This book is a very good read as it is an eclectic collection of essays written by international leaders associated with the Peter Drucker Foundation. Some key authors include: Senge, Moss Kanter, and Hesselbein himself as president of the Drucker Foundation. Readers will see where corporate America has learned valuable lessons from the newer sciences.

Jaworski, J. (1996). *Synchronicity: The inner path of leadership.* San Francisco: Berrett-Koehler. Perhaps the most inspirational book of the list, Joseph Jaworski takes the reader on a personal journey of self-destruction and subsequent enlightenment. From this individual introspection, we are then led through a litany of global-level web of leader relationships. Jaworski is uniquely able to show how one person can make a difference and how powerful leaders are making a difference.

McGreal, I. (Ed.). (1995). *Great thinkers of the eastern world.* New York: HarperCollins. Numerous scholars of Eastern philosophy have compiled an amazingly comprehensive series of biographical sketches of the *Great Thinkers of the Eastern World.* Philosophers from China, India, Japan, Korea, and The World of Islam are featured. It's incredible to read how these great minds intuitively knew the lessons that would some day be discovered by the new sciences.

Pine, R. (2000). *Science and the human prospect.* Belmont, CA: Wadsworth. Ronald Pine provides excellent diagrams to show many of the theoretical concepts taught in quantum physics. This is an outstanding read to quickly grasp these various principles. Pine does a superb job of providing examples and metaphors that help the reader understand both the theoretical and actual experiments.

Prigogine, I., & Stengers, I. (1984). *Order out of chaos.* New York: Bantam Books. This book is more technical than many of these other books, but is clearly a worthwhile read. Nobel laureate Ilya Prigogine and Isabelle Stengers begin with an historical look at the sciences and their relative impact on society. They finish with a thorough description of the new chemistry and its importance for today and tomorrow.

Schwartz, G., & Russek, L. (1999). *The living energy universe: A fundamental discovery that transforms science and medicine.* Charlottesville, VA: Hampton Roads Publishing. This entertaining and quick read provides compelling evidence for systemic and universal memory and for living energy in every thing. Gary Schwartz and Linda Russek begin with a neatly packaged parallel history of science and religion throughout the world. Also, they truly help to put some of the principles of quantum physics in the words of the layman.

Senge, P. (1990). *The fifth discipline: The art and practice of the learning organization.* New York: Doubleday/Currency. *The Fifth Discipline* is universally accepted as a book to be in every leader's personal library. Peter Senge brings forth his insights as to how organizations and their leaders can support their workers in order to both meet their needs and become highly effective at the same time. Again, this is yet another book that shows the interrelationships between people and between organizations and their environment.

Sergiovanni, T. (1990). *Value-added leadership: How to get extraordinary performance in schools.* New York: Harcourt Brace Jovanovich. Thomas Sergiovanni has spent his entire career espousing the moral responsibilities of educational administrators. His call for value-added leadership touches the inner core of all readers. Not only is he able to eloquently describe his working philosophy, he also provides excellent examples. This short book should certainly be required reading for all future leaders.

Shlain, L. (1998). *The alphabet versus the goddess: The conflict between word and image.* New York: Penguin Group. Leonard Shlain takes the reader through a very thought-provoking trip through history. His thesis is that in preliterate societies women played a more dominant, or at least equal role, in society. This is due to the fact that the predominate mode of communication is oral and comes from right-brained thinking. Over time, societies learn the linear, mechanistic mode of communication of writing—a left-brained and male-dominant approach. These dual ways of communicating have had a major impact on our societies and give us a new perspective of how we became who we are today.

Spears, L. (Ed.). (1998). *Insights on leadership: Service, stewardship, spirit, and servant leadership.* New York: John Wiley & Sons. Like any book by Robert Greenleaf, this book based upon his work should be considered a primary read for all people in leadership positions. This particular book is a conglomeration of chapters written by contemporary leaders who are associated with the Robert Greenleaf Foundation.

Waldrop, M. (1992). *Complexity: The emerging science at the edge of order and chaos.* New York: Simon & Schuster. Michael Waldrop does an excellent job of weaving together a set of stories of how some very excellent world-class scientists have come together at the Santa Fe Institute in Los Alamos, New Mexico. These scientists have been working, and continue to work, on the new science of complexity and how it relates to a thorough understanding of the global economy, technology, politics, and organizations.

Walker, E. (2000). *The physics of consciousness: Quantum minds and the meaning of life.* Cambridge, MA: Perseus Books. Walker provides a thorough description of the development of classical, and then quantum, thought throughout the ages. From this extensive introduction, Walker then describes or explains the implications of the observer and consciousness on the science. This analysis is crucial when we attempt to discern objective reality in our organizations.

Wheatley, M. (1994). *Leadership and the new science: Learning about organizations from an orderly universe.* San Francisco: Berrett-Koehler. This book should be a primer for anyone learning about or practicing management or leadership. It is significant because it is an easy read to get acquainted with quantum physics and some of the other new sciences as they inform administration in general. Wheatley eloquently breaks down the technical language for the lay person and provides dynamic examples throughout.

References

Abbott, J., & Ryan, T. (November 1999). Constructing knowledge, reconstructing schooling. *Educational Leadership, 57* (3), 66–71.

Amoroso, R., & Martin, B. (1995). Modeling the Heisenberg Matrix Quantum coherence and thought at the holoscape manifold and deeper complementarity. In King, J., & Pribram, K. (Eds.), *Scale in conscious experience: Is the brain too important to be left to specialists to study?* (pp. 351–357). Mahwah, NJ: Lawrence Earlbaum.

Batten, J. (1998). Servant-leadership: A passion to serve. In L. Spears (Ed.), *Insights on leadership: Service, stewardship, spirit, and servant leadership* (pp. 38–53). New York: John Wiley & Sons.

Block, P. (1996). *Stewardship: Choosing service over self-interest.* San Francisco: Berrett-Koehler.

Bolman, T. & Deal, L. (1995). *Leading with soul: An uncommon journey of spirit.* San Francisco: Jossey-Bass.

Bransford, J., Brown, A., & Cocking, A. (Eds.) (1999). *How people learn: Brain, mind, experience, and school.* Washington, DC: National Academy Press.

Capra, F. (1996). *The web of life: A new scientific understanding of living systems.* New York: Anchor Books Doubleday.

Champawat, N. (1995a). Rabindranath Tagore. In I. McGreal (Ed.), *Great thinkers of the eastern world* (pp. 260–264). New York: HarperCollins.

Champawat, N. (1995b). Sarvepalli Radhakrishnan. In I. McGreal (Ed.), *Great thinkers of the eastern world* (pp. 279–283). New York: HarperCollins.

Chomsky, N. (2000). *Chomsky: On miseducation.* Lanham, MD: Rowman & Littlefield Publishers.

Covey, S. (1990). *The seven habits of highly effective people.* New York: Fireside of Simon & Schuster.

Csikszentmihalyi, M. (1990). *Flow: The psychology of optimal experience.* New York: HarperCollins.

Darling-Hammond, L. (Spring 1999). Target time toward teachers. *Journal of Staff Development, 20,* 31–36.

Dolan, P. (1994). *Restructuring our schools: A primer on systemic change.* Kansas City, MO: Systems and Organizations.

Fassel, D. (1998). Lives in the balance: The challenge of servant-leaders in a workaholic society. In L. Spears (Ed.), *Insights on leadership: Service, stewardship, spirit, and servant leadership* (pp. 216–229). New York: John Wiley & Sons.

Feldman, D. (1994). *Beyond universals in cognitive development.* Norwood, N.J.: Ablex.

Gardiner, J. (1998). Quiet presence: The holy ground of leadership. In L. Spears (Ed.), *Insights on leadership: Service, stewardship, spirit, and servant leadership* (pp. 116–125). New York: John Wiley & Sons.

Gelatt, H. (January 1995). Chaos and compassion. *Counseling & Values, 39* (2), 108–116.

Gilman, R. (Winter 1993). The next great turning, *In Context, 33,* 11–12.

Gleick, J. (1987). *Chaos: Making a new science.* New York: Penguin Books.

Glickman, C., Gordon, S., & Ross-Gordon, J. (1998). *Supervision of instruction: A developmental approach.* Boston: Allyn and Bacon.

Goldsmith, M. (1996). Ask, learn, follow up, and grow. In F. Hesselbein, M. Goldsmith, & R. Beckhard (Eds.), *The leader of the future: The Drucker Foundation* (pp. 227–237). San Francisco: Jossey-Bass.

Goswami, A. (1996). Creativity and the quantum: A unified theory of creativity. *Creativity Research Journal, 9* (1) 47–61.

Gould, L. (1995). Quantum dynamics and neural dynamics: Analogies between the formalisms of Bohm and Pribram. In King, J., & Pribram, K. (Eds.), *Scale in conscious experience: Is the brain too important to be left to specialists to study?* (pp. 339–348). Mahwah, NJ: Lawrence Earlbaum.

Habito, R. (1995). Nishitani Keiji. In I. McGreal (Ed.), *Great thinkers of the eastern world* (pp. 395–398). New York: HarperCollins.

Handy, C. (1996). The new language of organizing and its implications for leaders. In F. Hesselbein, M. Goldsmith, & R. Beckhard (Eds.), *The leader of the future: The Drucker Foundation* (pp. 3–9). San Francisco: Jossey-Bass.

Heskett, J., & Schlessinger, L. (1996). Leaders who shape and keep performance-oriented culture. In F. Hesselbein, M. Goldsmith, & R. Beckhard (Eds.), *The leader of the future: The Drucker Foundation* (pp. 111–119). San Francisco: Jossey-Bass.

Hesselbein, F. (1996). The "how to be" leader. In F. Hesselbein, M. Goldsmith, & R. Beckhard (Eds.), *The leader of the future: The Drucker Foundation* (pp. 121–124). San Francisco: Jossey-Bass.

Hesselbein, F., Goldsmith, M., & Beckhard, R. (Eds.). (1996). *The leader of the future: The Drucker Foundation.* San Francisco: Jossey-Bass.

Hoy, W., & Miskel, C. (1982). *Educational administration: Theory, research, and practice.* New York: Random House.

Jaworski, J. (1996). *Synchronicity: The inner path of leadership.* San Francisco: Berrett-Koehler.

Kaku, M. (1997). *Visions: How science will revolutionize the 21st century.* New York: Bantam Doubleday Dell Publishers.

Kotter, J. (1999). *What leaders really do.* Cambridge, MA: Harvard Business School Press.

Lipman-Blumen, J. (1996). *The connective edge: Leading in an interdependent world.* San Francisco: Jossey-Bass.

Mandl, A., & Sethi, D. (1996). Either/or yields to the theory of both. In F. Hesselbein, M. Goldsmith, & R. Beckhard (Eds.), *The leader of the future: The Drucker Foundation* (pp. 257–263). San Francisco: Jossey-Bass.

Mansfield, V., & Spiegelman, J. M. (1996). On the physics and psychology of the transference as an interactive field. *Journal of Analytical Psychology, 41,* 179–202.

McConnell, J. (1980). *Understanding human behavior.* New York: Holt, Rinehart and Winston.

McGreal, I. (Ed.). (1995). *Great thinkers of the eastern world.* New York: HarperCollins.

McGregor, D. (1960). *The human side of enterprise.* New York: McGraw-Hill.

McGuire, M. (1991). *An eye for fractals: A graphic and photographic essay.* New York: Addison-Wesley Publishing.

Moss Kanter, R. (1996). World class leaders: The power of partnering. In F. Hesselbein, M. Goldsmith, & R. Beckhard (Eds.), *The leader of the future: The Drucker Foundation* (pp. 89–98). San Francisco: Jossey-Bass.

Palmer, P. (1998). Leading from within. In L. Spears (Ed.), *Insights on leadership: Service, stewardship, spirit, and servant leadership* (pp. 197–208). New York: John Wiley & Sons.

Palter, R. (Ed.). (1970).*The annus mirabilis of Sir Isaac Newton, 1666–1966.* Cambridge, MA: MIT Press.

Peitgen, H.-O, & Richter, P. (1986). *The beauty of fractals: Images of complex dynamical systems.* Heidelberg, Germany: Springer-Verlag.

Pine, R. (2000). *Science and the human prospect.* Belmont, CA: Wadsworth.

Pollard, C. W. (1996). The leader who serves. In F. Hesselbein, M. Goldsmith, & R. Beckhard (Eds.), *The leader of the future: The Drucker Foundation* (pp. 241–248). San Francisco: Jossey-Bass.

Prigogine, I. & Stengers, I. (1984). *Order out of chaos.* New York: Bantam Books.

Pritchett, P. (1994). *The employee handbook of new work habits for a radically changing world: 13 ground rules for job success in the information age.* Dallas: Pritchett & Associates.

Rettig, P. (Spring 2001). Can you quantumfy that? *Educational Considerations, 28,* (2), pp. 11–15.

Rettig, P. (Fall 2000). Leslie's lament: How can I make teacher supervision meaningful? *Educational Horizons, 79,* (1), 31–37.

Rettig, P. (November 1999). Differentiated supervision: A new approach. *Principal, 78,* (3), 36–39.

Rudd, L. (June 17, 2001). The day-to-day movements of Wall Street are random, unpredictable. *Oshkosh Northwestern.* p. C.2.

Schwartz, G., & Russek, L. (1999). *The living energy universe: A fundamental discovery that transforms science and medicine.* Charlottesville, VA: Hampton Roads Publishing.

Senge. P. (1996). Leading learning organizations: The bold, the powerful, and the invisible. In F. Hesselbein, M. Goldsmith, & R. Beckhard (Eds.), *The leader of the future: The Drucker Foundation* (pp. 41–57). San Francisco: Jossey-Bass.

Senge, P. (1990). *The fifth discipline: The art and practice of the learning organization.* New York: Doubleday/Currency.

Sergiovanni, T. (1990). *Value-added leadership: How to get extraordinary performance in schools.* New York: Harcourt Brace Jovanovich, Publishers.

Sergiovanni, T., & Starratt, R. (1993). *Supervision: A redefinition.* New York: McGraw-Hill.

Shim, J-R. (1995). Chinul. In I. McGreal (Ed.), *Great thinkers of the eastern world* (pp. 407–412). New York: HarperCollins.

Shlain, L. (1998). *The alphabet versus the goddess: The conflict between word and image.* New York: Penguin Putnam.

Spears, L. (Ed.). (1998). *Insights on leadership: Service, stewardship, spirit, and servant leadership.* New York: John Wiley & Sons.

Stapp, H. (1993). *Mind, matter, and quantum mechanics.* New York: Springer-Verlag.

Taubes, G. (May 1996). Schizophrenic atom doubles as Schrodinger's Cat— or kitten. *Science, 272,* 1101.

Tucker, M. (1995). Nakae Toju. In I. McGreal (Ed.), *Great thinkers of the eastern world* (pp. 351–354). New York: HarperCollins.

Tucker, R. (May 1983). "Ilya Prigogine: Wizard of time." *Omni*, 84–121.

Ulrich, D. (1996). Credibility X capability. In F. Hesselbein, M. Goldsmith, & R. Beckhard (Eds.), *The leader of the future: The Drucker Foundation* (pp. 209–219). San Francisco: Jossey-Bass.

Vitiello, G. (1995). Dissipation and brain. In King, J., & Pribram, K. (Eds.), *Scale in conscious experience: Is the brain too important to be left to specialists to study?* (pp. 381–403). Mahwah, NJ: Lawrence Earlbaum.

Waldrop, M. (1992). *Complexity: The emerging science at the edge of order and chaos.* New York: Simon & Schuster.

Walker, E. (2000).*The physics of consciousness: Quantum minds and the meaning of life*. Cambridge, MA: Perseus Books.

Weber, G. (1996). An "outsider's" view on leadership. In F. Hesselbein, M. Goldsmith, & R. Beckhard (Eds.), *The leader of the future: The Drucker Foundation* (pp. 293–302). San Francisco: Jossey-Bass.

Wheatley, M., & Kellner-Rogers, M. (September 1996). Breathing life into organizations. *Public Management (US), 78* (9), 10–15.

Wheatley, M. (1994a). *Leadership and the new science: Learning about organizations from an orderly universe*. San Francisco: Berrett-Koehler.

Wheatley, M. (October 1994b). Quantum management. *Working Woman, 19* (10), 16–17.

Wheatley, M. (1993). *Leadership and the new science*. Videorecording and Instructor's Manual. Carlsbad, CA: CRM Films.

Wilson, K., & Daviss, B. (1994). *Redesigning education*. New York: Henry Holt.

Wolf, F. (1994). *The dreaming universe*. New York: Simon & Schuster.

Wolf, F. (1988). *Parallel universes: The search for other worlds*. New York: Simon & Schuster.

Yam, P. (June 1997). Bringing Schrodinger's Cat to life. *Scientific American,* 124–129.

Zukav, G. (1980). *The dancing Wu Li masters: An overview of the new physics*. New York: Bantam.

Index

Abbott, J., and Ryan, T., 100, 121
Amoroso, R., and Martin, B., 68, 101, 121
Anaxagoras, 36
Arthur, B., 56

Barnard, C., 8
Batten, J., 58, 121
behaviorism, xii, 3, 6, 22, 25, 100
Bell, J., 42, 83
Bell's Theorem, 42–45, 60, 83–84, 88, 94
Benard cells, 59–60, *60*, 85–86
Benard, H., 59–60
Block, P., 7, 21, 24, 25, 47, 80, 117, 121
Bohm, D., 22, 55
Bohr, N., 37, 39, 40
Bolman, T., and Deal, L., 13, 18, 103–4, 121
Bransford, et al., 6, 7, 12, 98, 101, 121

Capra, F., xii, 35, 47, 49, 53, 59, 60, 62–63, 72, 84, 96, 117, 121
Carroll, P., 73
Champawat, N., 29, 46, 121
chaos theory and the science of complexity, 53–58, 84–85, 90; *See also* glycerine experiment

Chinul, 1
Chomsky, N., 12, 104, 121
classical physics. *See* Newtonian physics
Clauser, J., and Freedman, S., 42
complementarity principle, 37, 38, 39, 82, 87–88, 97
Confucius, 46, 64
constructivism, 100–2
Covey, S., 4, 24, 47, 58, 121
Csikszentmihalyi, M., 46, 47, 64, 117, 121

Darling-Hammond, L., 25, 98, 105, 122
dissipative structures and chemical clocks, 58–64, 85–86; *See also* Benard cells; vortex
Dolan, P., 23, 24–25, 47, 80, 89, 97, 99, 102, 117, 122
double-slit experiment, 36–40, *38*, 82, 94; *See also* complementarity
Drucker, P., 105
dynamic systems theory. *See* chaos theory

Eastern philosophy/religion, 46–47
Einstein, A., ix, 75, 93
Eldridge, N., 57
Eliot, T. S., 107

Palmer, P., 85, 123
Palter, R., 4–5, 123
Peitgen, H., and Richter, P., *69, 70,* 123
Perry, T., 49
Pine, R., 37–39, *38,* 40, 42–44, 45, 47, 82, 90–91, 102, 118, 123
Pollard, C., 97, 123
Prigogine, I., and Stengers, I., ix, 15, 55, 56, 58, 59, 60, 63, 85, 86, 118, 123
Pritchard, D., 41
Pritchett, P., 86, 123

quantum physics, x, 34, 90–91; appropriate application of, 45–48; budgeting, as it relates to, 102–3; curriculum and instruction, and assessment, as it relates to, 100–102; definition, xi, 35; key principles, 35–37, 110–11; lessons, 87–91, 108–9, 113–15; model of leadership, xii, 34; organizational structure, as it relates to, 96–98; the quantum school, 103–5; supervision and evaluation, as it relates to, 98–99
quantum tunneling, 40

Radhakrishnan, S., 46
Rettig, P., 12, 87–91, 115, 124, 127
Rudd, L., 56, 124

The Santa Fe Institute, 56–57
Schrodinger, E., 40–41, 83
Schrodinger's cat, 40–42, 44–45, 83, 94
Schwartz, G., and Russek, L., 34, 65, 101, 118, 124
Senge, P., 5–6, 26, 46, 47, 73, 119, 124

Sergiovanni, T., 21, 22, 24, 45, 119, 124
Sergiovanni, T., and Starratt, R., 9, 124
Sheldrake, R., 64–65
Shim, J., 1, 124
Shlain, L., 3, 34–35, 39, 67, 119, 124
Skinner, B. F., 3, 6
slime mold cycle, 72–73, *72,* 87
Spears, L., 119, 124
Stapp, H., 3, 35, 124
systems thinking, xii, 47

Taubes, G., 41, 124
Taylor, F., 4, 6–7, 105
Theory X and Theory Y, 8–9
Toffler, A., 15, 58–59
Toju, N., 46, 64
traditional physics. *See* Newtonian physics
Tucker, M., 64, 124
Tucker, R., 85, 86, 124

Ulrich, D., 105, 124
uncertainty principle, 40

Vitiello, G., 58, 96, 101, 124
vortex, 60–62, *62,* 85

Waldrop, M., 56, 57, 67, 88, 119, 124
Walker, E., 40, 42, 101, 119–20, 125
Watson, J., 3, 6
Weber, G., 25, 98, 125
Western Electric Hawthorne Studies, 8
Wheatley, M., ix, 4, 22, 26, 34, 35, 40, 44, 46, 47, 55, 62, 67, 71, 75, 89–90, 96, 102, 104, 110–11, 120, 125
Wheeler, J., 45

Wilson, K., and Daviss, B., 100, 125
Wolf, F., 5, 101, 125

Yam, P., 41, 125

Young, T., 42

Zukav, G., 40, 42, 44, 45, 54, 67, 82–83, 101–2, 125

About the Author

Perry R. Rettig has served as a classroom teacher in grades four through eight and as a principal in both elementary and middle school settings. He earned his master's degree in educational administration and leadership from the University of Wisconsin-Milwaukee and his Ph.D. in educational administration and leadership from Marquette University.

Currently, Rettig serves as an associate professor of educational leadership at the University of Wisconsin–Oshkosh where he serves as coordinator of the program. He teaches courses in the supervision and evaluation of teaching, the organization and administration of educational systems, educational leadership, professional staff development, and the principal internship. His scholarship has focused primarily on the newer sciences and how they can provide insights into school system reform.